GRAY DAYS and GOLD

Sea Witch

GRAY DAYS and GOLD

A Character Sketch of Atlantic Mutual Insurance Company

Compiled and edited by John N. Cosgrove
Illustrations by Gordon Johnson
Privately printed for the Atlantic Companies

Copyright 1967 by the Atlantic Companies

DESIGNED AND PRODUCED BY DOREMUS & COMPANY
Printed in the United States of America

Preface

In the days when the proud sails of American packets and clipper ships whitened every sea, Atlantic Mutual was founded as a marine insurer.

Since then, for a century and a quarter, all the men who have steered the company's course have been linked by principle in the performance of the promises behind Atlantic policies.

A chain of integrity unbroken for 125 years is cause for pride. But this story of the company is neither an exercise in self-satisfaction nor a recital of uninterrupted triumphs, for in the long years in which it has been growing up with our country, Atlantic has sailed through both "Gray Days and Gold." The color and variety of these days and the exciting events that marked them form the basis of this narrative.

It is not intended as a definitive history of the company nor as a chronological record but as a character sketch of an institution that has endured because of the dedication of the men who have managed its affairs through the years—the trustees and the officers. The true significance of the events chronicled herein therefore lies in their revelation of the characters of the men who brought them to pass or who were affected by them.

Each wave of company management faced challenges peculiar to its own era. Some of Atlantic's leaders did not advance its fortunes on the tides of change and progress. They were content to keep the company afloat while preserving its principles and values. Fortunately, stronger successors renewed the company's momentum and growth.

In 1853, the first president of Atlantic said: "It has been and will be my desire to conduct the company so as to satisfy the expectations of all reasonable men, and so that all those friends who feel a particular interest in it may be proud of it; and with the patronage of those who established and sustained it, and favored by that Great Power governing both the winds and the sea, I hope for at least a moderately favorable result hereafter."

His hopes have not been disappointed.

And yet, it must be remembered that this record of 125 years really marks a point of departure for a long voyage into a new insurance world of tomorrow.

Those who will command Atlantic's fortunes on that voyage can embark with the confidence born of the heritage left them by their predecessors: Constancy of purpose carried out by men of character. No better sailing orders could be handed down.

Acknowledgments

Acknowledgment is due to the official and personal reminiscences of four of Atlantic's presidents: William D. Winter, J. Arthur Bogardus, Franklin B. Tuttle and Miles F. York.

In addition, the *Disaster Books* of the company provided a rich source of background material, as did the *Atlantic Log*, the company's official publication, and its editor, Celia Lambert.

The title of this work is taken from a felicitous phrase of William D. Winter, seventh president of the company. In his reminiscences of his career with the organization, Mr. Winter referred to "...The Atlantic Mutual Insurance Company, where for almost half a century, through Gray Days and Gold, I have lived my business life." No choice of words could have more aptly expressed the varying fortunes of the company throughout its long history.

Contents

A Tradition Begins	13
Growing with the Country	28
Transition to Tragedy	39
A New Leader and New Problems	44
Constancy through Crisis	51
A Half Century of Progress	62
New Era; Old Leaders	73
Crises: World War and Depression	88
The Winter-Bogardus Years	98
Modernizing the Business	109
Times Change—Traditions Endure	115
Challenge and Opportunity	133

List of Illustrations

Sea Witch	Frontispiece
The Great Chase for the Whale	*opposite* 16
The Ship That Nearly Burned Down New York	*opposite* 32
The Agreement That Kept Union Shipping under Sail	*opposite* 48
Last Victory of the C.S.S. *Shenandoah*	*opposite* 56
The Loss of New Bedford's Whaling Fleet	*opposite* 64
Sighting the Ghost Ship *Mary Celeste*	*opposite* 80
The *Titanic*	*opposite* 96
Studying the *Disaster Books* in Atlantic's Marine Library	*opposite* 112
The Presidents of Atlantic Mutual	*opposite* 128

FRONTISPIECE Built in 1846, just four years after Atlantic Mutual was founded, the *Sea Witch* was one of the most famous of the clipper ships. She regularly outsped competitors from New York around Cape Horn to San Francisco, and once made history by racing home from Canton, China, to New York in an incredible seventy-four days. Under the command of Captain Robert Waterman, she broke more speed records than any American ship of her size.

GRAY DAYS and GOLD

A Tradition Begins

In 1842 South Street in New York City was one of the most exciting thoroughfares in the world. It was the center of shipping in the world's second busiest seaport.

Bobbing at South Street piers were the vessels of shipowners whose captains barked commands on the stormy Atlantic, off the languid isles of southern seas, off Cape Horn, off the Cape of Good Hope—in fact, wherever the trade routes led.

The ships that came to harbor in South Street loaded tea, silks and spices at Canton; went rolling down to Rio for coffee; picked up cotton at New Orleans; stowed lumber on board at Savannah and brought home fortunes in cargo from other ports around the world.

The bowsprits and jib booms of these vessels speared far across the cobbled roadway of South Street until it seemed they would poke into the windows of the countinghouses of the merchants and fleet owners across the way. Beneath this forest of spars, the wharves were laden with cotton bales, kegs of rum, plump bags of sugar, boxes filled to bursting with textiles. Some of this unending inventory would be hauled to nearby warehouses on drays drawn by snorting horses or rolled there on hand barrows by dock workers. The rest of the pile of rich stores would be swung aboard ships bound for faraway ports.

New Yorkers crowded South Street in those days, drawn by the fragrant odors of tar, Norway pine and exotic spices; by the wheezing of donkey engines; the creaking of windlasses and the hair-curling oaths of stevedores and truckmen.

Excitement mounted as the bustling crew of a merchant ship made ready for departure. Spectators delighted in the sailors' sea chanteys—cheerful, rollicking songs unlike anything ever heard elsewhere. There was no particular sense to the words, but the sails went up as if by magic when the chanteymen led the refrain:

> *Then up aloft that yard must go*
> *Whiskey for my Johnny!*
> *Oh! whiskey is the life of man,*
> *Whiskey Johnny!*
> *I thought I heard the old man say*
> *Whiskey for my Johnny!*

Why this particular ballad became an outstanding favorite when the clippers ruled the seas is a mystery. According to Valentine's *Manual of Old New York,* the crews of American clippers for many years carried no grog aboard—in contrast to the ships of almost every other nation—and served only hot coffee to the watch even in Antarctic waters.

This policy may or may not have been a factor in the success of the clippers. But at one time marine insurers, guided by their experience with these fleet vessels, made standing offers to other types of merchantmen of a discount of 10% if coffee were quaffed aboard instead of liquor.

The climax of an exciting day on the East River front came when a ship was finally made ready and was tugging at her moorings. With the tide ebbing and the white sails glistening, the anchor was brought to the rail, head sheets began to draw and the ship gathered way in the slack water. The ensign was dipped, and the graceful clipper, with a smother of foam at her forepeak, was away for the Golden Gate and the perils of Cape Horn.

Many ladies in the colorful costumes of the era graced the scene on sailing day, especially young matrons with children who would profit by the living lesson in geography and commerce that was South Street.

The sightseeing ladies had more to do with the shipping business than they perhaps realized. Canny merchants and fashion makers had seen to it that more and more cloth was added each year to the female costume. By the 1850s the average dress comprised 30 yards of material, while the numerous petticoats and other undergarments, discreetly unmentioned, brought the total to an astounding 100 yards. Since the trade of New York port depended largely on textiles—raw or transformed into finished products—the voluminous feminine fashions were not so flighty as they seemed. They added to rapidly growing profits.

But the ladies had their critics. An English newspaperman of the era accused them of enlarging and modeling their lovely forms to the beau ideal of female beauty by means of "bustles, cushions, plaiting, stuffing, puffing, and other devices." This writer was concerned about the deception to his fellow males, especially anyone who married a lady "inflated into symmetry."

Ungallantly, the critic made a strong case for such a hapless groom: "Might he not demand an annulment of the marriage contract? Might he not plead that he had been cheated and deceived? Might he not say, 'I married, as I thought, a fine robust, well-formed woman. I find her, divested of her borrowed plumes and stuffing, an ordinary feeble-bodied object as shapeless as a post.'"

The merchants and shippers of New York surely had little sympathy with this complaint about feminine duplicity. They liked to see living evidence of their thriving trade in dry goods, and they welcomed the ladies to South Street, even though these paragons of fashion were not there on formal business.

One person who was there for that purpose on the morning of June 27, 1842, was E. C. Powell, Esq., a New York merchant. Nestled among the hundreds of hulls at the piers was his schooner, the *A. F. Thorne*. Mr. Powell had to tend to a few details at a countinghouse. These out of the way, he charted his course west from South Street for 47 Wall

one of the first organizations in the country to write marine insurance. His ability and integrity soon became known in the business, and he was invited to join the Pacific Insurance Company of New York as its secretary. At this early point in his career, young Jones conceived a lifelong aversion to litigation over claims. He had observed that much of it was unnecessary and irksome. More important, litigation often proved detrimental in the end to insurance companies. It was a sure way to drive customers away. A sounder procedure was to select risks carefully in the first place and to deal fairly and promptly with claims when they arose.

Thus, determination to keep out of legal wrangles was a fixed precept with Jones when he moved in 1824 to the new Atlantic Insurance Company—a stock organization. His position was assistant to the president, the equivalent of a vice-presidency today. The president of the company was Archibald Gracie, a substantial merchant, whose country seat on the East River near Hell Gate is now known as Gracie Mansion, the home of New York's mayors.

Regrettably, 1824 proved to be a bad year to start a marine insurance company. In their anxiety for business, the companies had begun to cut prices and by 1825 they were in a full-scale rate war. Losses were mounting at the same time. The combination was fatal, and many insurers went out of business.

The first Atlantic Insurance Company did not fail. Instead, the company wisely suspended writing in 1826 and petitioned the New York legislature for the right to dissolve and liquidate after payment in full of all claims and debts. The legislators granted permission in 1828, and the Atlantic, after making good on all its obligations, paid its stockholders a dividend of 53%. Its charter was kept in force.

The company's dissolution was based on the management's early recognition that money could not be made in the prevailing economic climate. The liquidation was not only prudent but honorable, for in the same act in which it permitted the company to dissolve, the legislature authorized the directors to raise new capital. They determined to make a fresh start under the improved conditions of 1829.

The legislature approved new capital of not less than 5,000 shares nor more than 10,000 with a par value of $50. The old stockholders were favored by the first offering. At once, 7,000 shares were subscribed, 3,000 in Boston and the remainder in New York and vicinity.

Mr. Gracie did not continue as the head of the changing Atlantic organization. Other employees had been given separation allowances. But Walter R. Jones was still prominent in the picture.

Joining him in the management of the second Atlantic Insurance Company was Josiah L. Hale of Newburyport, Massachusetts. He had begun his career in Boston as office boy in the Merchants' Insurance Company. Later he became secretary of the Washington Marine Insurance Company, and, when that insurer opened a New York City branch, it sent young Hale down as manager. His friendship with Jones began soon after his arrival. Their relations were harmonious, and they were an ideal team to conduct the affairs of the second Atlantic.

Hale had raised the capital and was named president. Jones was the assistant or vice-president. However, their status was equal. Both received an annual salary of $2,000.

In December, 1829, the revived organization began business with the same name and the same charter. The faith of the directors—25 outstanding business leaders—was immediately justified. Business flourished and by June of 1830 the company declared a dividend of 5% to the shareholders. The organization prospered for twelve-and-a-half years. In that time, those who held its stock received dividends of 436½%. This is equal to a yearly rate of 35%—a figure to excite the envy of present-day management in insurance or in any other business.

In May of 1842 another move for dissolution was made. But this time the reason was quite different. The clearest explanation of the maneuver is given by William D. Winter, seventh president of Atlantic Mutual (1934-1946), in his classic book, *Marine Insurance:*

"During the twenty years immediately preceding the Civil War, and while the prosperity attending overseas commerce due to the clipper ships was at its height, a curious situation developed in the marine insurance market. Many shipowners were also merchants, and many merchants either owned or partially owned ships. It seemed to them that to the profits they made from their trading ventures they could add profits which some companies were making on the insurance of these ventures. They accordingly began to organize mutual marine insurance companies and to pay off stockholders and change stock companies into mutual companies. These men were rugged individualists—capitalists who wished to gain as much of the profits arising from their overseas ventures as was possible. However, they were also willing to accept the losses inherent in venturing, if fate should so decree."

This move into the insurance business by shipowners was a striking example of the leadership of merchant-venturers in establishing the investment process in this country. The point is emphasized by John Chamberlain in his book *The Enterprising Americans,* published in 1961 by Harper & Row:

"It was commerce that provided the vital capital needed to stimulate and expand domestic United States manufacturing and businesses of all kinds. With money made out of the China trade, Stephen Girard of Philadelphia moved into banking, offering in 1812 a complete service under one-man management. Money made by the Browns of Providence out of foreign trading, and by the Lowells and Jacksons of Boston and Newburyport, Massachusetts, out of shipping spilled over into textile manufacturing. So, too, did the whaling money of New Bedford, Sag Harbor and New London. In the 1830s and 1840s came the really dramatic shifts. For example, John M. Forbes took his own capital won in the China trade and with a number of merchant friends bought into the unfinished Michigan Central Railroad. John P. Cushing, a mercantile agent at Canton, put his money into banks, insurance companies and railroads, most of them in New England. Thus the original merchant capital became the first investment capital in the New World. It had all come out of the sea."

Chamberlain recalls that George Washington was an eminent merchant. His wheat was famous as the source of superfine flour produced by his own mills and sent across the seas in barrels made at his own cooperage plant. He became the biggest flour producer in the Colonies, gaining most of his cash income from three mills, which enabled him to produce for markets as far away as the West Indies. He was also a leading exporter of tobacco. The profits from Washington's trading were invested in real estate and made him one of the wealthiest men in 18th-century America.

However, because of the Revolution, loans to the government, unreliable Continental currency, and enormous personal expenses,

Washington fell heavily into debt and by the end of his life he was in financial difficulties.

After the Revolution—in the late 18th century and well into the 19th—there was a shortage of American capital, and there was no beneficent power beyond the seas to supply it. The new nation had to store up its own reserves of money and energy for new and risky ventures and to rely on its own inventiveness to expand and develop its infant industries.

Nothing could have been accomplished without the merchant-shippers who furnished the capital to get the investment process going. "Trading up" had always been congenial business to the colonists, especially the New Englanders, and the visible sign of their success was the acquisition of gold and silver specie from abroad. United States reserves of specie, at first desperately short, increased by 1820 to a point that permitted the Federal Government to pay off most of its foreign creditors in hard coin.

The first big "breakthrough" voyage had come as early as 1784 when the *Empress of China* sailed out of New York Bay for Macao and Canton. This pioneer venture into the China trade set the pattern for the new order of merchants. The profits on this voyage were $30,000 or 25% on the capital, and when the report was published, it started other risk takers on the road to the East.

This trend culminated in the 1850s when the clippers reached the peak of their glory. Meanwhile, typical American traders were sending merchandise all over the earth. They stocked every market. They created wants in order to supply them. They covered the New Zealander with Southern cotton woven in Northern looms, built blocks of stores in the Sandwich Islands, swapped with the Fiji cannibals, sent whaleships among the icebergs of the poles and made life tolerable in the dwellings of the Indian jungles. They became not only merchants of consequence but the managers of investment funds.

Typical of this venturesome breed were the men Winter describes as anxious to add insurance to their other interests in the two decades before the Civil War. They were intent on converting Atlantic to a mutual company, for this meant that as policyholders they would share in the profits that went to shareholders under the stock type of operation.

Jones was aware of the trend to the mutual system from its beginnings. However, he realized that while all progress involves change, all change does not result in progress. He cautiously watched developments in moves from the stock to the mutual principle. Satisfied that the procedure was sound and would succeed, he and President Hale called a meeting of their shareholders to sell them the idea of converting to a mutual organization.

This was not a simple task; Atlantic stock owners had been realizing average dividends of 35% a year. Understandably then, there was opposition to the proposed plan. But Jones and Hale must have been persuasive. The motion was carried by 3,149 shares in favor to 1,421 against. The company ceased to accept new risks, and the second Atlantic closed its books.

A new chapter in the history of the organization—the one with which this narrative is concerned—thus began on April 11, 1842, when the New York legislature granted a charter to the Atlantic Mutual Insurance Company. This included the right to issue not only marine policies but also fire and life insurance. Present officials of the company have wistfully speculated on what that broad charter would mean to the organization today. However, charters in 1842 were granted for a maximum of thirty years, and on subsequent renewals, the fire and life powers of the Atlantic were not maintained. In any case, marine insurance was the business in which the company was rooted, and it was the important line of those early days.

In the new enterprise, Jones became president and Hale took the title of assistant. The agreeable relations between the two men may be judged by a unique plan on which they agreed. Jones was to be president one year, Hale the next, and so on, alternately. This was never put into effect. Hale's health was uncertain, and he chose to remain in the secondary role.

Without discredit to Hale, it may fairly be said that Jones's permanent role as president was fortunate for the organization. In the book *The Rise of New York Port*, written by R. G. Albion and published in 1939 by Scribner's, there is a comment on Atlantic Mutual:

"The company's success can be attributed in no small degree to the superlative genius of a Long Islander, Walter Restored Jones, who was easily the outstanding figure in New York marine insurance."

Such was the background and management of the organization at 47 Wall Street, where E. C. Powell, New York merchant, turned in on June 27, 1842. He doffed his beaver hat, carefully set his walking stick aside, responded to the dignified greetings of the officials of the new company and sat down with them to transact his business.

By the light of sperm candles, he signed his name to a document. Within minutes he was the owner of the first policy written by Atlantic Mutual. His pleasure was matched by that of the company's officials. Since the records show that the transaction was completed at noon, it is not unlikely that they went out in company to take luncheon and perhaps a glass of wine at one of the sumptuous restaurants in the neighborhood. Such a pleasant interlude would have been a fitting climax to an historic event, for Mr. Powell will forever stand at the head of an endless procession of Atlantic policyholders.

That procession was not long in forming. In fact, even earlier, at a meeting of the trustees in May, 1842, applications for $800,000 in insurance had been received, although the policies were not immediately issued. Many of the applications came from the trustees—the outstanding merchants, shipowners and civic leaders of the day—who were eager to patronize their own company and to profit from the mutual operation. Their reputations for financial acumen brought other customers to the new enterprise.

Even a brief review of the careers of a few of the first Atlantic trustees is sufficient to show that they were in the grand tradition of the merchant-entrepreneurs who put down the foundations of American prosperity.

All the trustees were enterprising individualists and none more so than Thomas Tileston of Boston. A printer's devil at age thirteen, he advanced to editor of a Haverhill, Massachusetts, paper, the *Merrimack Intelligencer*. In 1818 he became a commission merchant in New York. His firm of Spofford and Tileston developed an export-import trade with South America and the West Indies and maintained its own sailing fleet. Two of the organization's ships, *Southerner* and *Northerner*, plied between New York and Charleston and are believed to have been the first two coastal steamships in the United States.

Tileston and his partner later bought the Dramatic Line of sailing packets, which they operated profitably into the 1860s. The firm was among the first to rush gold seekers to California after the strike at Sutter's Mill and to bring back rejoicing miners who had struck it rich in their venture.

Sitting with Tileston at early meetings of Atlantic trustees was William F. Havemeyer, Jr. An outstanding success in sugar refining, he was able to retire from active business at thirty-eight. In 1845 he became mayor of New York, under the banner of Tammany Hall. Later, he came back to haunt that organization.

Havemeyer served a second term as mayor and remained prominent in politics throughout the War between the States but then dropped out of public affairs until the early 1870s when he was outraged by the brazen plundering in New York by the Tweed Ring. He joined Governor Samuel T. Tilden and a committee of leading citizens in cleaning up the city and chasing Boss Tweed out of the country. Havemeyer was an uncomfortable man to have on one's trail, as Tweed could attest. Experience in business, coupled with his terms as mayor with the backing of the same Tammany Hall that Tweed had later captured, enabled Havemeyer to go directly to the banks and books where Tweed's graft and corruption were recorded with devastating accuracy.

In 1872, Havemeyer again became mayor—this time as a Republican. He died in office after notable accomplishments in civic reform during his long career, although his last term was marred by political wrangling.

Another colorful figure at Atlantic's first trustee table was Jonathan Goodhue of Salem, Massachusetts. Son of a United States senator, he was trained in a Salem countinghouse and had made voyages to the Far East as a supercargo before coming to New York to form his own commission house. In 1834, he bought the Black Ball Line, a famous fleet of packet ships out of Liverpool.

Goodhue's transactions were worldwide. His firm enjoyed the highest standing and had strong backing in London financial circles. By 1848, its net worth was $7 million.

A fellow Yankee and trustee, George Griswold, had much in common with Goodhue in the way of enterprise. He came to New York from Connecticut in the late 1790s and set up an import house with his brother, Nathaniel. Their ships, laden to the limit with flour, regularly reached the West Indies and came home with rum and sugar. Later, the Far East attracted the brothers, and they became leading tea importers. The Griswolds owned a fleet of clippers, including the legendary *Panama*, which knew few equals in its day.

John Cleve Green, another trustee, left his native New Jersey to begin his career as a supercargo on a Griswold ship and showed his good sense later by marrying George Griswold's daughter. However, he also demonstrated his independence by leaving the Griswolds to go with the great merchandising house of Charles H. Russell in Canton. Within a year he was head of the firm at thirty-four. Green amassed a sizable fortune trading in tea and textiles. In 1839 he returned to the United States. He and another former Russell partner then took over the Michigan Central Railroad. Green amassed a fortune of millions, part of which he donated to Princeton University in his native state. He was a principal benefactor of that leading institution.

Other original trustees of the company brought to the new organization solid if less romantic backgrounds—all calculated to inspire confidence. William C. Pickersgill, for example, was a prosperous banker with headquarters at 49 Wall Street, next door to Atlantic Mutual. Augustin Averill was a distinguished merchant in New York and a trustee of The Seamen's Bank for Savings, which is still a neighbor of the insurance company.

From the beginning, the quality of the men on Atlantic Mutual's board of trustees has been one of the company's bulwarks. The names of those who have helped guide the organization add up to a roster of luminaries in American business and public affairs for a century and a quarter.

Among other early trustees was Franklin H. Delano, whose grandnephew and namesake, Franklin Delano Roosevelt, was President of the United States from 1932 to 1945. Mr. Delano was a partner in the importing house of Grinnell, Minturn & Co.

The Grinnell brothers of New Bedford, Massachusetts, stemmed from a firm of whale oil commission merchants. Later, they were among the leading merchants and packet operators in New York. Their firm owned two ship lines, and their house flag flew over more than fifty vessels. In addition, they operated general freighters and the most famous of the clippers, the *Flying Cloud*. Cornelius Grinnell was an Atlantic Mutual trustee from 1853 to 1868.

The Low family of Salem, Massachusetts, destined to make its mark in American business, politics and education, contributed two outstanding trustees to Atlantic, Abiel A. Low and his brother, Josiah O. Low. In 1829 their father, Seth Low, had moved his business in Chinese and Indian drugs from Salem to Brooklyn, New York, where Abiel soon joined him. Later, Abiel went to Canton, gained experience, and in 1840 set up on his own in the China trade in New York. Other members of the family, including his son, Seth—named for his grandfather—entered the enterprise. On the first round trip of their clipper *Surprise*, from New York to California, the Lows cleared a sizable profit.

The Low clippers and those of other American owners came into competition with the British merchant marine in the treaty ports of China. Crack British East Indiamen waited for cargo weeks on end while one American clipper after another sailed with a cargo of tea at double the ordinary freight. When the Lows' *Oriental* arrived in London, ninety-seven days out of Hong Kong, crowds thronged the docks to admire her, and the London *Times* challenged British shipbuilders to set their skill, industry and dogged determination against the youth, ingenuity and ardor of the United States.

After his notable career in commerce, the younger Seth Low became president of Columbia University and mayor of New York City and of Brooklyn, then a separate city.

But perhaps the most remarkable story of Atlantic trustees is the saga of the Dodge family—a name that has been connected with the company for 120 years.

This tale has its inception in a career that might have provided the pattern for the plots of Horatio Alger, chronicler of the lives of poor boys who made good. Anson G. Phelps of Simsbury, Connecticut, typified the industry and virtues of Alger's heroes.

Left an orphan as a young boy, he learned the saddlery trade, set up a business in Hartford and began to sell his products in the South. He came to New York in 1812 and formed a partnership with Elisha Peck of Hartford. Soon they were engaged in the importation of iron, copper, brass and other metals, an activity in which Phelps was acknowledged as the leader. To pay for these commodities abroad, he shipped cotton from New York and was one of the promoters of a pioneer line of coastal packets to Charleston.

Dissolving his partnership with Peck, Anson Phelps took two of his sons-in-law into the firm. One was William E. Dodge, a native of Connecticut, who got his start as a $3-a-week clerk in a New York dry-goods concern. Later, after operating a country store back in Connecticut, Dodge established himself as a dry-goods jobber in New York before marrying one of Phelps's daughters and becoming a partner in the metal business.

Eventually, Phelps Dodge Corporation, one of the brightest names in American industrial lore, supplemented the importation of metals by developing a domestic supply of iron from western Pennsylvania and copper from Michigan and Arizona, as well as engaging in the manufacture of metal wares, particularly in the Connecticut town of Ansonia, named for Anson G. Phelps. Both he and William E. Dodge became noted for their support of religious and philanthropic endeavors.

William E. Dodge became a trustee of Atlantic in 1847 and continued until his death in 1883. From the day he attended his first meeting 120 years ago, there has been a member of his family at the company's trustee table, save for a short lapse of two years. His son, William E. Dodge, Jr., succeeded him as a trustee in 1883 and remained until 1903. In 1905 Cleveland H. Dodge, his son, resumed the traditional seat.

This third-generation Dodge, who remained on the board until 1925, was a Princeton classmate and lifelong friend of Woodrow Wilson. During World War I he gave to war-relief agencies all the personal profits he had realized from government patronage of his firm during the conflict.

Cleveland E. Dodge, son of this illustrious father, replaced him on the board of Atlantic Mutual in 1925. He was for many years vice-president of Phelps Dodge Corporation, which today mines and refines copper and turns that vital metal into the wire and cable that are the lifelines of American industry.

Mr. Dodge typifies the modern businessman. Yet his career is in the individualistic pattern of Atlantic's pioneer trustees. After graduation from Princeton he traveled in the Near East and the Far East. Then for five years he worked at manual and engineering tasks in the copper company's mining camps in Arizona, New Mexico and Mexico. He spent six months in 1916 with the U. S. Army on the Mexican Border and was an officer in a field artillery unit throughout World War I. When his regiment was disbanded in 1919, he went to work at Phelps Dodge headquarters in Arizona. In 1920 he returned to the New York office. He was elected a vice-president in 1924 and a director in 1926. As Atlantic Mutual approached its 125th anniversary, Mr. Dodge still graced the company's board of trustees. Thus, a member of the family has helped to guide the company's affairs from the days of the clipper ship to the space age—a record surely unique in American business.

Growing with the Country

The path taken by E. C. Powell, Atlantic's first policyholder, from South Street to the company's first offices in the old Merchants' Exchange Building at 47 Wall Street, soon became a popular route. In his wake followed shipowners, resplendent in their Prince Alberts and beaver toppers. Often accompanying the owners and at other times acting for them were sea captains who transacted business in voices better attuned to the quarter-deck than to the underwriting room.

However, both owners and masters were made to feel at home in Atlantic's candlelit headquarters. Set out on a sideboard for their refreshment was a generous wheel of sharp cheese and mounds of crackers. Happily ignorant of calorie counting, the visitors, whose figures often billowed fore and aft, hacked ample wedges of cheese and conducted negotiations between bites. The formal binding of a risk was often signalized by the applicant's rising and brushing a few stray crumbs from his formal or seafaring garb.

Welcoming the merchants and captains in the early days were Walter Restored Jones, Josiah Hale and the small clerical staff. They were soon joined by John Divine Jones, nephew of the first president, who was named secretary in the fall of 1842. His career with the company was to span fifty-three years, forty of which he served with distinction as its president.

The procession of customers in the summer of 1842 and the mounting stacks of policies bolstered the confidence of the officials and trustees in the soundness of their venture. It is doubtful that their faith would have been shaken even had they known that every other mutual marine insurer—and there were close to fifty established between 1820 and 1850—would ultimately founder. Atlantic's leaders had organized the company on the basis of their own experience and vision. They were aware that it would have to ride out commercial squalls and storms, but they never doubted that it would prosper and endure.

Confidence was a primary requisite for any businessman starting an enterprise in the 1840s. John Tyler, unflatteringly called the first "accidental" President of the United States because he took office in 1841 on the death of William Henry Harrison, the hero of Tippecanoe, was struggling to lead the young country of some 20 million out of the deep depression that had started in 1837. The panic, largely due to wild land speculation as the nation moved westward and to excessive state debts and expansion of credit, did not reach its low point until 1843, and the country did not regain overall prosperity until 1845.

Thus, while confidence was indispensable in starting a new venture, that quality would have been fatal without the foresight that characterized Atlantic's founders. They looked far beyond the immediate and based their hopes on facts that led to an enlightened assessment of the future. They envisioned New Frontiers long before that inspirational phrase gained popularity almost 120 years later.

One hard and comforting fact was the $800,000 in applications for insurance the company had immediately received when it began operations. The merchant-applicants, including Atlantic's own trustees, daily took the pulse of world trade, and their desire for coverage was a sound indication that the import-export business would flourish despite the domestic depression. They did not misread the signs; events justified their judgment.

Another factor in the calculated optimism of the company's officials was the continuing improvement in the speed of sailing vessels that was to culminate in the golden age of the clipper ship from the 1840s into the 1860s. The term "clipper"—derived from the phrase "going at a fast clip"—had first been used just before the War of 1812. At that time, the long, low, rakish schooners built on Chesapeake Bay were dubbed "Baltimore Clippers." They were small, heavily masted and with little carrying capacity. The first classic clipper, the *Ann McKim,* a three-masted vessel with square sails on every mast, was built in Baltimore in 1832. In the following decade, giant clippers began to float majestically out of New England yards.

While their cargo capacity was limited in relation to their size, they could show their heels to any ship on the seas. Where sailing vessels formerly took from 150 to 200 days for the New York to San Francisco run, the new ships could make it in less than 100 days. The *Flying Cloud,* most famous of them all, set a record of 89 days and 9 hours for her proud owners, the Grinnell brothers.

They were fortunately spared the knowledge that their superb ship would end her career in humiliation when the days of sail were over. She became a New Haven scow and was regularly towed up and down Long Island Sound with brick and concrete for cargo. From the stack of the tug towing her, clouds of filthy smoke blew back on the once beautiful queen of the seas.

The clippers were the most glamorous and exciting of all vessels, but the durable sailing packets had long been the chief vehicles of American shipping. These sturdily constructed ships plied the Atlantic on shuttle runs for many years, carrying passengers and cargo. In the era when Atlantic was founded, the packets were attaining their maximum in speed and size.

Meanwhile an even more significant marine development was taking place: Steamships were coming into their own. Back in 1819 the *Savannah* had been credited with the first Atlantic crossing under steam. However, she had used her steam for only 80 hours of the

29 day-11 hour crossing from the city for which she was named to Liverpool. It was not until 1838 that permanent steam service on the Atlantic was established. On April 23, the *Sirius* and the *Great Western* put into New York harbor within several hours of each other.

Two years later, Samuel Cunard's steamers were on a permanent run from England to Boston, and in 1848 he extended his service to New York. Meanwhile, numerous competitors were vying with him on the Atlantic. By 1860, many of the steamships had cut their ocean crossing time in half. Paradoxically, the death knell was sounding for the fleet clippers and the doughty sailing packets even while they were reaching the days of their greatest fame.

In any case, the pace of shipping and merchandising was virtually doubled in the early years when Atlantic was intent on gaining commercial momentum. In this development, Atlantic officials foresaw endless possibilities for the expansion of profitable commerce that they were only too willing to underwrite.

Fortune favored the young company in many other ways. In 1844, the United States made a treaty with China, permitting lucrative trade with a number of ports in addition to Canton. Trade with the Hawaiian Islands boomed and accelerated when California came into the Union in 1850. Commodore Perry's bold foray to the front door of Japan released the pent-up commerce of that formerly mysterious land.

The Crimean War and the Sepoy Mutiny preoccupied England and benefited American shipping when the British for a time depended on other maritime nations to transport much of their commerce. Meanwhile, the continuing gold rush to California—the greatest human migration since the Crusades—brought a bonanza of premiums to Atlantic, although later there would also be some tragic losses. The California gold strike and another in Australia not only expanded shipping through the carrying of passengers and goods to and from those regions but increased the supply of specie and enlarged the purchasing power of the United States and other countries. This, in turn, stimulated further economic development and commerce.

While most of these events were still in the making, the officers and trustees of Atlantic already had tangible evidence that their company was well on the way to success. Early in 1844, they took a look at results and concluded that the gratifying profits would justify a dividend of 40% to the policyholders. But with the prudence that was to characterize the management through the years, they held the payment to 35%, issued in the form of scrip certificates. These, in effect, were notes payable to the holders and redeemable at the option of the company. As time went by, the certificates were generally called at the end of five years. Meanwhile they returned interest at the annual rate of 6%.

This conservative method of operation gave the company a constant backlog of unpaid dividends represented by the scrip. The funds due the policyholders were used as operating surplus—a stable financial basis for the enterprise.

Word of Atlantic's profitable experience and of the rewards realized by its policyholders was not long in sweeping through Wall Street and the business community. Since success is the most potent form of advertising, Atlantic attracted new customers and its volume was accelerated.

Alert insurance leaders were soon aware of this rapid but sound growth. John Correy Smith, president of Insurance Company of North America—founded in Philadelphia in 1792—judged the new venture to be the strongest of the New York insurer operations. Accordingly, in April of 1844, he wrote to President Jones: "This company has been in the practice of effecting reinsurance to a considerable extent. Under these circumstances, it has occurred to us that we might establish a correspondence with your company which would prove mutually advantageous.

". . . Should you be disposed to reinsure for us, the risks we would offer would be principally by inland transportation, to and from New Orleans, and to and from Brazil."

The 2-year-old Atlantic accepted this proposal from the 52-year-old Philadelphia company. This was the beginning of an association that has spanned 123 years—surely one of the most enduring relationships in the history of insurance or of any other commercial enterprise.

Atlantic was literally "growing up" with its home city—a struggling community that did not even remotely suggest the metropolis it was destined to become. It was not until 1844, when James A. Harper

Christmas festivities were barely over in 1853 when a raging fire swept through buildings on the East River front of New York City. The *Great Republic*, America's largest clipper ship, was soon enveloped in flames. Ships berthed fore and aft ignited. The inferno threatened the area from Wall Street to City Hall before the last flames were quenched nearly four days later. Atlantic carried $197,000 on hulls and cargoes, according to the *Disaster Books*.

of the famed publishing firm was elected mayor, that a uniformed police force was established. The uniforms were adorned with copper buttons, and the proud wearers were soon known as "cops"—an appellation that endured.

Mayor Harper also set up a contract street-cleaning service and barred from the thoroughfares the roving pigs that formerly played a leading role in this vital function. To bring added dignity to the city, particularly to Atlantic's neighborhood, the mayor ruled that cattle could no longer be driven downtown below 14th Street.

So many major developments marked the country's progress during Atlantic's formative years that any attempt to describe the company's growth with a panorama of American history as a background would be superficial. However, in Atlantic's earliest days, striking advances in many fields seemed directly designed to aid the company's fortunes.

Sitting in the Supreme Court room in the United States Capitol in Washington in 1844, Samuel F. B. Morse tapped out the first telegraphic message across the miles to Baltimore: "What Hath God Wrought?" His invention revolutionized communications, laced the country together and speeded up transactions in every phase of business. Years later, the most famous symbols of Morse's ingenious code, S O S, would avert many disastrous marine losses for Atlantic. At other times, when the plea for help came too late, the grim letters would signalize another entry in the company's *Disaster Books*.

Another genius, Charles Goodyear, patented his process for the vulcanization of rubber in the same era. He did as much as any man to put America on wheels, but it is doubtful if many insurers writing automobile business in the 1960s, including Atlantic, would regard his contribution as an unmixed blessing.

The first rotary printing press began to produce newspapers and other forms of printed matter more speedily and efficiently in 1847. The Pennsylvania Railroad was chartered. Elias Howe devised the first sewing machine with an eye-pointed needle. Commerce, communications and manufacturing were thus revolutionized at the very time Atlantic was putting down foundations for the future. The march of events carried the company along.

However, in addition to benefiting from the development of other enterprises, Atlantic contributed substantially to their progress. From its earliest days, the company's investments have reflected changing economic conditions and the management's sagacity in placing its funds in ventures destined to grow and endure.

For example, in 1844 when Atlantic was becoming firmly established, the leather trade flourished in lower New York City. The company invested in the shares of Leather Manufacturers National Bank. The first purchase was modest—only 100 shares. But in 1904 this bank merged with Mechanics National Bank, of which Atlantic had been a shareholder since 1855. As the years passed, these two organizations were involved in other mergers, and the original investment in Leather Manufacturers eventually became part of the stock of Chase Manhattan Bank—a security that is prominent in Atlantic's portfolio today.

In 1855, Atlantic bought its first shares of The Bank of New York stock. Through the years the holdings were increased. This security, still on Atlantic's books, is now worth more than seven times its cost to the company, and its return in a year is 27% on the investment.

These two examples of bank stocks—one held for 123 years and the other for 112—illustrate the company's policy of staying with sound basic investments in good times and bad—through booms, panics, recessions and depressions. This practice matches Atlantic's unwavering adherence to its philosophy of underwriting operations, which the investment function has always supported.

Atlantic's early momentum was not halted even by the war with Mexico, which exploded in 1846 after a long wrangle over the annexation of Texas and the extent of its boundaries. At the outbreak of hostilities, President Jones immediately called a meeting of Atlantic's trustees and arranged to assume war risks.

The conflict had little or no effect on premium income, but Atlantic's losses were heavier than anticipated. The scrip dividend declared in 1847 was therefore reduced to 12% with the usual 6% interest.

The Mexican army was crushed in 1847, and the war was soon forgotten, for in 1848 James W. Marshall found gold on the property of John A. Sutter while building a sawmill on the south fork of the American River not far from Sacramento, California. The news brought hundreds of thousands, "bit by the yellow fever," racing to

San Francisco. Sailing vessels of every description from large ocean-going ships, barques and brigs to small coastal cutters, brigantines and schooners arrived in California, every inch of available space crammed with gold seekers and goods. Back at 47 Wall Street, Atlantic's underwriters pored over the ceaseless stream of applications for coverage on the gold fleet.

The avalanche of business from the gold strike and from the general prosperity of the country was soon reflected in Atlantic's personnel. By 1850 the clerical staff had grown to fourteen men. President Jones was then confronted with his first major employee-relations problem.

The frock-coated clerks, squinting under the guttering candlelight, were hard put to ply their quill pens speedily enough to register the insurance written, to record the losses and to keep the company's accounts. They decided to petition Jones for the installation of gas fixtures on their desks. Their plea was shrewdly worded:

"Aside from the injury to our eyes from the constant flickering of the lights from candles, it is believed that after the first cost of the pipes, a great saving could be effected in the cost of lights by the use of gas in lieu of candles, and that this would tend much to our convenience in performing our duties."

Added to his customary concern for the welfare of his staff, this hint that the company would benefit was irresistible to Jones. The gas was installed with an injunction that the jets were to be turned off when the employees were leaving the building. The president's own light was usually the last to be extinguished. He customarily appeared at the office before 8:30 A.M. and often did not leave until nearly midnight.

Even so, there were not enough hours in the day to enable the president to deal with all his problems. They were unending and of a bewildering variety. For example, a relentless toll of shipping was being taken in the waters of Hell Gate, a turbulent stretch of the East River about midway between Upper New York Bay and Long Island Sound, and running from what is now 90th Street to 100th Street.

This channel was choked with rocks, some approaching the size of small islands. During the Revolution a British frigate, the *Hussar*, had struck a rock near Hell Gate and had sunk so rapidly that the cargo of several million in gold, which she was carrying to pay the Redcoats, could not be saved. That treasure has presumably remained buried in East River mud to this day, for the swift current frustrated repeated efforts at salvage.

In Atlantic's early years, the heavy maritime traffic to and from New England sustained severe losses as vessels were caught up in the vicious East River swirl and tossed like toys until their hulls and bottoms were smashed. Skilled navigators of the Hell Gate Pilots Association had to take the wheel from the regular helmsmen when ships approached this deadly area.

To make matters worse, pirates lurked offshore and plied a profitable trade. It seems incredible but for many years in the last century, buccaneers had a hideout on Big Mill Rock, not a half mile from where today's East River Drive winds its way past Gracie Mansion and the luxurious residences of one of New York's most exclusive sections. The marauders swarmed aboard ships that were staggering through Hell Gate, attacked the crews and made off with valuable cargo.

In 1851, New York City appropriated approximately $14,000 to make the channel safe. The merchant Henry Grinnell, a partner of Grinnell, Minturn & Co., and a brother of Cornelius Grinnell, an Atlantic trustee, was especially determined to get rid of the infamous Pot Rock on which many a vessel had come to grief. He engaged Benjamin Maillefort, a contractor, and agreed to pay him $5,000 for clearing the rock to a depth of 24 feet below the mean water level.

Later in the year, Atlantic made the first of a number of contributions to the effort to remove the jagged threats to navigation. Throughout 1852 the company advanced additional sums until it had an investment of about $3,000 in the project. This was to be paid back by Congress with interest, if and when it made an appropriation for this purpose, or by New York State. Congress did appropriate $20,000 in 1853, but Atlantic's records do not disclose when the money was repaid.

Hell Gate proved to be a formidable foe. The blasting of stubborn boulders from its angry waters continued at intervals until the late 1880s when U. S. Army engineers dynamited many of the largest hazards out of the river. By this time the battle with the resistant rocks had become a form of entertainment for New Yorkers who gathered on nearby shores to view the spectacular geysers of water and rock set off by the engineers. Several times in 1885 *The New York Times* carried front-page stories and charts showing how the Army was finally winning the battle with Flood Rock, Mill Rock, the Gridiron and Bald Headed Billy, which had for so long made Hell Gate a stony passage of death.

When the dynamiting ceased, many New Yorkers missed the excitement, but Atlantic officials were relieved and never regretted that the company had done its part in getting rid of so serious a menace to shipping.

As Atlantic's business boomed and its staff increased, the cramped quarters in the Merchants' Exchange proved inadequate. The trustees, therefore, asked the finance committee to find a suitable site for a new building that would accommodate current needs and allow for future expansion. Their selection was admirable. They bought choice lots on the southwest corner of Wall and William streets—the site of the present Atlantic building. The members of the finance committee did not strike quite as good a bargain as the Dutch had in acquiring all of Manhattan Island for $24, but they had no cause to be apologetic. The cost of the lots and of the new building when completed in 1851 was $267,447.45. Today, the same Wall Street corner and the Atlantic Building, which rises there, are among the most valuable properties in New York City.

Established in its new home, Atlantic marked its 10th anniversary in April, 1852. Total profits for the decade amounted to more than $4.9 million on premium income of about $23 million. Losses paid had been $8.5 million. Moreover, in 1851, the company surged past the $2 million mark in volume and in 1852 added another million. Profits on 1852 business alone came to more than $1 million. These achievements were in marked contrast to the results of the years immediately preceding Atlantic's 125th anniversary, when underwriting profits eluded most companies.

Understandably pleased by the record, the trustees were generous in their praise of the efforts of the executive officers and staff. They gave the major credit to President Jones, and they decided to honor him for his management of their affairs.

The trustees planned a fitting tribute—a civic dinner at the Astor House, then on Broadway across from City Hall Park. A notable company of his friends and colleagues assembled there on November 22, 1853, to honor Walter Restored Jones and to witness the presentation to him of an enduring testimonial: A service of silver plate inscribed with sentiments that permanently linked his name with that of the company.

The most gracious tribute of the evening was paid by William E. Dodge, trustee and pioneer member of the firm of Phelps Dodge Corporation. Noting that Jones was a bachelor, Mr. Dodge observed that while the president would not leave children of his own, generations of commercial "descendants" in Atlantic's service would honor his memory.

The president responded with equal felicity, but he was more realistic than the trustees in discerning the basic reasons for Atlantic's growth:

"We have assembled here at a very auspicious period: Tranquil at home and at peace with all the world. Prosperity has spread over our land. The great staples of the country—cotton, grain and gold—are abundant. The capacity of our merchant marine is now estimated at 4.5 million tons. Our ships visit every accessible port. Their sails whiten every sea. They obtain full employment.

"In conducting this great and growing commerce, insurance is deemed indispensable and receives the ready support of our merchants."

The ceremonies in Jones's honor ended on this optimistic note.

Transition to Tragedy

Unhappily, President Jones's optimism was shattered within a few weeks when a series of calamities struck the company, presaging the worst year in its history, which was to come in 1854.

Between Christmas of 1853 and the New Year, New York City was enjoying its most peaceful annual period. But, in that week, a raging fire swept through buildings on the East River front. The streets and docks were an inferno of burning brands. As if in conspiracy against marine insurers, the conflagration crackled toward their prime risks.

The *Great Republic,* the largest merchant ship ever constructed in the United States or elsewhere until that time, was soon enveloped in flying sparks and then in licking tongues of flame that toppled her masts. She became a charred hull and was scuttled with her cargo of beef, lard, wheat, corn, flour, cotton, tea, rosin, tobacco, and maple and cedar wood.

The hapless *White Squall,* moored at a nearby pier, was set afire by brands from the dying *Great Republic.* The smaller vessel was cut adrift and let go before the wind to save other ships at the dock. Residents of Brooklyn stared helplessly as the floating mass of flame crossed the river and neared their shore. She touched there, a skeleton, her days in the California and China trade finished forever.

Meanwhile, the *Joseph Walker,* a new packet loaded with cotton, grain and rosin for Liverpool, had ignited simultaneously with the *Great Republic* and had burned to the water's edge for a total loss.

Atlantic's *Disaster Books* show that the company had a total of $197,000 at risk on the hulls and cargoes of the three vessels. But this was not the end. Another entry reveals that on the same disastrous day the mail steamship *Winfield Scott,* bound for Panama from San Francisco, went aground at Santa Barbara. Atlantic's share of that loss was $35,000.

These December tragedies brought drastic confirmation of the growing loss trend that had begun earlier in 1853. At the annual meeting in January, 1854, the trustees concluded that the pattern of events dictated a lower-than-usual dividend of 16% with the regular 6% interest on the scrip.

Early in the year, Josiah Hale decided that his failing health would no longer permit him to carry on in an increasingly arduous business. He resigned as vice-president and trustee and returned to his native Newburyport, Massachusetts. Had he remained with Atlantic through the turbulence of 1854, it is speculative whether he would have survived another twenty years, as he did in retirement. John Divine Jones succeeded Mr. Hale and became the right-hand man of President Jones.

A succession of smashing gales began in January, 1854. Impartial in their choice of victims, the winds took a toll of a large number of ordinary freighters and a prime selection of crack members of New York's fleet of steamships, packets and clippers.

Atlantic's early success had been tied to the clipper ship, but in 1854 these white swans of the seas seemed determined to drag the company down with them to watery graves around the world. The *San Francisco,* insured by Atlantic for $254,000, was ravaged by raging Pacific gales and windswept waters. She drifted, as if seeking haven at home, to the entrance of the port for which she was named and sank there. Another clipper, the *Trade Wind,* was lost in a collision at sea, and the famous *Oriental,* owned by the Lows, went down in Chinese waters. The payments on these two vessels came close to $70,000.

Steamship risks added to the drain on Atlantic funds. The *Franklin* of the Havre Line ran ashore on Long Island. Atlantic had $20,000 on the hull and $176,000 of the $472,000 coverage on the cargo, part of which was recovered. Another $54,000 was lost on the cargoes of two British steamers of the Inman Line.

Three ocean-sailing packets—the Red Star Line's *Waterloo,* given up as missing; the Swallowtail Line's *Prince Albert,* abandoned at sea; and the Black Ball Line's *Montezuma,* wrecked on Long Island—represented another $80,000 in company commitment.

Atlantic also came to grief on inland waters. On the Ohio River, some $55,000 worth of coal went down when barges sank. And out in the North River, almost in sight of Atlantic's offices, the caloric engine steamer *Ericsson,* chugged on a trial run, encountered a squall, capsized and went under. Atlantic paid $50,000 on this vessel, the brainchild of John Ericsson, who later built the *Monitor,* which was to help save the Union Navy from threatened destruction by the ironclad *Merrimac.*

Altogether the company's losses for the year came close to $4.5 million, far exceeding the premiums.

When the trustees met in January, 1855, the solemn atmosphere was in sharp contrast to their previous sessions. They were aware that every wave of prosperity has its reacting surge, but this philosophic consideration was no guide to immediate action. The trustees were, above all, practical men with their focus on the future.

They were told by their examining committee that the maritime disasters of the past year were the worst in the commercial history of the world. The committee observed, however, that Atlantic's record had been better than that of other marine insurers. Despite this partial reassurance, the trustees decided to pass the dividend. Their regret in being forced to take this action would have been tempered had they known that this first withholding of payments to policyholders would also be the last. Atlantic has never since failed to pay a dividend.

The trustees adjourned their meeting with understandable forebodings of continued disasters at sea. Fortunately, these fears were to prove groundless. But another type of disaster was to strike the company—one which the trustees did not foresee.

To them Walter R. Jones had appeared to be his usual vigorous self, though understandably disturbed by the appalling results of the past year. But the extent of his concern was far greater than anyone suspected.

The abrupt change in Atlantic's fortunes after more than a decade of success and the consequent failure to reward policyholders with a dividend were crushing developments for Jones. Although he continued for long hours at his desk, his health and spirit were impaired. He left his office on April 6, 1855, at 9 P.M., and died of a stroke the next morning at his home on Murray Street in New York.

Before noon of April 7, every flag on Wall Street was at half-mast. As the sad news spread, South Street merchants also lowered their banners. For the next several days marine insurance men—competitors as well as colleagues—recounted Jones's contributions to their craft. The merchants of the city recalled the part he had played in the expansion of American and world commerce by underwriting their ventures and equitably settling their claims.

In the funeral cortege passing through lower New York to Trinity Church at the head of Wall Street was the Chamber of Commerce—the leading businessmen of the city—marching in a body. Accompanying them were civic dignitaries and the employees of Atlantic.

At the funeral, in a day given to unabashed expression of sentiment, there was no lack of eulogy. But the most enduring estimate of the character of Walter R. Jones lies in two continuing organizations. The first is a commercial enterprise—Atlantic Mutual itself. The principles Jones established for its conduct still guide the company's management.

The second organization is the Life Saving Benevolent Association—a humanitarian group of which Jones was the founder in 1849 and president until his death.

He formed the association to give succor to those shipwrecked in the heavy marine traffic of Long Island Sound and off the New Jersey coast. The United States Coast Guard was not established until 1915, and the United States Revenue Cutter Service, founded in 1790, did not usually provide lifesaving services. Moreover, the United States Life Saving Service was not organized until 1871. Therefore, the private Life Saving Benevolent Association built small boat houses at strategic points from which lifeboats could reach the stricken. The rescue houses were also equipped with cannon to shoot lines to the wrecks and to allow those on board to reach land by means of an all-enclosed metal car. From one ship, the *Ayrshire*, 200 passengers were brought safely ashore in this manner.

The association saved countless others from drowning or freezing to death in the winter months. Through its long history, except for a period of a few years, this humane organization has always been led by the current chief executive of Atlantic Mutual.

But as long as its benevolent work is continued, Walter R. Jones will be remembered as its first leader, just as he will always be preeminent in the history of Atlantic and of marine insurance in this country.

A New Leader and New Problems

After the disasters of 1854 and the death of its president in 1855, Atlantic's major need was an inspired leader who could lift it out of its temporary trough and restore it to the crest of commercial fortune. The trustees, who perhaps had been inclined to regard their first president as indispensable, discovered that John Divine Jones was uniquely prepared to take command. He had experience as an expert adjuster of losses and for a time as secretary of the rival Merchants' Marine Insurance Company. Most important, he had worked directly for close to thirteen years with his uncle, absorbing his underwriting acumen and practical business sense.

The trustees therefore confidently entrusted the direction of Atlantic to him in April of 1855 when they elected him president. John D. Jones's accession to office marked the beginning of a new era in Atlantic's history. It could hardly have been otherwise; the country itself was speedily nearing the most momentous years of its young life.

But the new president had a brief respite before he was called upon to guide the company through its most challenging period. As if in prophecy of a great career, Jones's first year in office was a bright one. Based on the 1855 results, the trustees at the annual meeting in 1856 brought the scrip dividend back up to 30% with the usual interest. At that meeting, William H. H. Moore, who had joined the company the year before, was elevated from third to second vice-president. His later promotions came much more slowly. Mr. Moore waited forty years until he became president, so it was fortunate that his career as an executive of the company had begun when he was only thirty-one years of age.

Jones himself was not quite forty-one when he became president, an unusual circumstance for those days and a most auspicious one for the company, for he brought to his post vigor and powers of imagination that might have been lacking in an older man. His imaginative and venturesome approach to company affairs was illustrated early in his career as president when he became involved in negotiations with a rather unusual person who had an intriguing idea for salvaging one of Atlantic's major losses.

This story began on the morning of September 8, 1857, when the Pacific Mail ship *Central America* strained at her Havana moorings as if impatient to cast off for New York. Although they were homeward bound, the gold miners crowding her decks and singing lustily saw no reason to change the verse they had roared to the tune of "Oh! Susannah" on their way out to California several years before:

> *Oh Californy!*
> *That's the land for me!*
> *I'm bound for Sacramento*
> *With my washbowl on my knee.*

These words had proved prophetic; the miners had struck it rich. Stashed below the decks of the *Central America* was some $1.6 million in gold they had sweated out of the California fields.

The singing did not last long. Off Cape Hatteras, the winds and the sea raged at the ship. Her seams opened wide and the water gurgled in, seeking the gold even more greedily than had those who had taken it out of the foothills of the Sierra Nevada.

On the night of September 12, after 152 persons had been rescued by other ships, the *Central America* went down with 423 of the passengers and crew; her gallant captain, William L. Herndon, U. S. Navy; and the treasure in gold.

Jones and his Atlantic colleagues were content to pay their share of the loss. With the cargo at the bottom of the ocean, they had no inkling that there would be a sequel to the tragedy.

However, on a summer's morning in 1858, President Jones had a visitor: Monsieur Brutus de Villeroi, late of Paris, but by then a U. S. citizen and a resident of Pennsylvania. The underwriting eye of Jones measured M. de Villeroi as something of a departure from the regular clientele of Atlantic. Jones mentally catalogued his visitor as a promoter, and so he was. Nevertheless, the president gave him an attentive and courteous hearing.

The intrepid de Villeroi proposed to raise the gold in the hulk of the *Central America* by means of his invention—a submarine. In return he was to be given 75% of all the gold recovered within a year. He had an agreement drawn to that effect between himself and parties with an interest in the gold. Seizing any opportunity to recover part of the loss for his policyholders, Jones immediately signed on behalf of Atlantic.

Regrettably, the story ends on an inconclusive note, for apparently the year went by without success. The *Disaster Books* of Atlantic simply record the loss of the *Central America*, its passengers, the crew and the gold. M. de Villeroi never found his way into those archives. The only record of his existence and of his proposal—novel for his day 109 years ago—lies in the company's copy of the agreement.

Jones, who signed the pact with the Frenchman, would undoubtedly have been delighted to deal with another de Villeroi—this one not a promoter, but a professional with the unromantic name of Vernon "Skinny" Parker—who played a similar but successful role in the affairs of Atlantic 104 years later.

In March of 1962, on the Mississippi near Memphis, the tug *Caleb H* was towing ten barges, five of them laden with $1,250,000 worth of blocks of lead, commonly called pigs.

For reasons that will always be known only to the pilot, the *Caleb H* smashed into a bridge pier, splitting the entire tow of barges in half and scattering them all over the river. The cargo of lead pigs began to drop off—piece by piece—until 1,404 blocks had found the Mississippi's muddy bottom.

There were witnesses to the accident, but, when an insurance investigation began, they were reluctant to talk. Those who make their living on Ol' Man River have always been clannish and disinclined to discuss with outsiders the faults of those whose livelihood is from the same source.

But after piecing events together and adding a few assumptions of their own, Atlantic's experts decided they had a good idea where the pigs had entered the water. It seemed reasonable that the best way to determine the approximate location of the lost lead was to repeat the accident—except for hitting the pier. A local river maintenance-and-repair firm was engaged to throw overboard a pig of lead with a cable attached. This sank in 86 feet of water and came to rest 6 feet down river. As a double check, the operation was repeated with the same result. Atlantic's men were then almost positive that the cargo was not far away from that spot.

After securing permission from the U. S. Coast Guard and the U. S. Army Engineers to start groping around the bottom of the river, the insurance representatives began looking for the rare individual who could retrieve the lead. Diving in the Mississippi is like sticking one's head in a bucket of mud—not too attractive a way of making a living.

However, in a small town somewhat inappropriately named Metropolis, Illinois, the salvage experts located "Skinny" Parker, one of the few deep-sea divers willing to transfer his trade to the muck of the Mississippi. He agreed to a test dive and found the lead exactly where Atlantic's men thought it was, piled neatly in three pyramid shapes ranging as high as 20 feet. After his test plunge, Parker, although not overly enthusiastic about the assignment, took it on.

Backing him up were tugs, a derrick boat, several work barges and miscellaneous equipment. Another deep-sea diver was engaged as a standby to come to Parker's rescue should he have trouble on the river's treacherous bed.

A month later, after perpendicular travels of 32 miles, the redoubtable Parker and his cohorts had recovered 1,398 pieces of the 1,404 lead blocks. The loss had cost five underwriters $257,000. Owing to a drop in market values between March and August, the lead was sold for $238,000. Atlantic had about 50% of the risk. The cost of recovery came close to $60,000.

Salvage has become a science since the visionary de Villeroi volunteered to plunge in his submarine to recover the *Central America's* gold. But he deserves a salute. He had his eyes on a worthwhile goal, and his aspirations represent a link with present-day recoveries such as the raising of the lead pigs from the Mississippi. In any case, the two episodes emphasize that the second president of Atlantic, John D. Jones, was as aware as the company's management is today of the importance of salvaging lost cargo for the benefit of its policyholders.

The sinking of the *Central America* was far from the most important problem presented to Jones in 1857. That year brought the worst financial panic to date in the country's history. About 5,000 business enterprises failed. Looking out of his office window at Wall and William streets, Jones had direct evidence of the seriousness of the crisis. Silk-hatted financial leaders, including Commodore Cornelius Vanderbilt, milled on the sidewalk with humbler citizens.

All had been caught when the New York branch of the Ohio Life Insurance & Trust Co. failed, triggering a disaster that had been in the making for some time. The underlying cause of the crisis was the watering and inflating of stocks by promoters so that securities had neither assets nor dividends to support the prevailing prices.

Long before the debacle, the economic community had been put on notice that it was pursuing a dangerous course. In 1853, George W. Curtis, editor of *Harper's*, wrote:

"The gold comes on in flood; steamships multiply week by week; banks rise up at street corners like Aladdin palaces; new stocks cumber the brokers' lists; new equipages throng the streets; new debts and profits quicken the stir of trade; and new churches—here and there—lift a warning finger of stone."

Only four years later, the warning was fulfilled. United States troops were marched up Wall Street, past Atlantic's offices, to guard the Custom House and the Subtreasury. Crowds broke into food shops and bakers' wagons to avert starvation. The depression lasted two years, and an additional 8,000 firms went under.

Jones's success in guiding the company in profitable operations

Confederate raiders, built and equipped in Great Britain, were devastating federal shipping. Seeking to reassure northern merchants and shipowners, President Lincoln met with Atlantic Mutual President John Divine Jones and promised him that if the company would provide war-risk protection, the United States would file claims against the Crown for reimbursement when hostilities ceased. Atlantic Mutual insured hundreds of merchant ships and whalers and by the end of the war had paid nearly 10,000 claims.

throughout this unsettled era may be judged by his report to the trustees early in 1861. He noted that at the end of 1860, after eighteen-and-a-half years of operation, the company showed an overall profit of $11,852,560. Its staff had grown to forty-six employees.

With all his primary responsibilities and problems in conducting the affairs of Atlantic, Jones was ceaselessly active in efforts on behalf of the maritime industry, the marine insurance business and allied interests. Thus, in 1860, at a preparatory meeting, he presented a plan for the organization of the American Shipmasters Association.

The purposes of this group could be set forth in long and prosaic detail. But they are much more vividly expressed in the dedication to the seventy-five-year history of the association, published in 1937:

> *They that go down to the sea in ships,*
> *That do business in great waters;*
> *These see the works of the Lord,*
> *And His wonders in the deep.*
>
> *The 107th Psalm of David*

"To protect such men and to preserve the property in their care was the primary incentive for the organization."

Jones took the lead in achieving these aims. Further organizational meetings were held during 1861, with the executives of nine other marine insurers participating. Of this original group, only the sponsor company, Atlantic, survives. American Shipmasters was chartered in 1862 and continues today as the American Bureau of Shipping.

From the inception of planning in 1860, Jones acted as chairman, and on the formal granting of the charter he became president, serving from 1862 to 1871. He was called back for another term from 1881 to 1886.

For 105 years the American Bureau of Shipping has collected and disseminated information on subjects of marine and commercial interest. For many years it ascertained and certified the qualifications of those seeking to be commanders or officers and encouraged the worthy among these applicants.

It has promoted the security of life and property on the seas through surveys and inspections. Finally, it has maintained a faithful and accurate classification and registry of mercantile shipping. All these activities mean that the organization has centralized efforts to aid and develop the U. S. Merchant Marine. The establishment and continued support of the bureau by Atlantic is one of the company's proudest contributions to America's maritime history.

Despite the growing success of the company, a pall hung over the 1861 meeting. The trustees and officers had very early foreseen the prospect of secession and even the possibility of civil war. Engaged as they were in world and domestic trade, they had a keen appreciation of the tragic potentials of such a conflict. Their forebodings had been confirmed a year earlier, when, with other leaders of New York City, they had heard Abraham Lincoln in his Cooper Institute address state that there could be no compromise on the question of slavery extension. Now, Lincoln was President of the United States.

His message had not been lost on Jones. The imminence of war had preoccupied him ever since he heard Lincoln speak. Thus, even before the first Confederate shell burst over Fort Sumter in April, 1861, he knew what Atlantic's role in the tragic struggle must be, and he was determined to fulfill it.

Constancy through Crisis

After the bombardment of Fort Sumter in April, 1861, a blockade was proclaimed against Georgia, Alabama, Florida, Mississippi, Louisiana, Texas, Virginia, and North and South Carolina. Eventually, more than 3,500 miles of coastline from Cape Henry to the Mexican border were to a greater or lesser extent sealed off. This merciless clamp-down, which grew from a loose to a tight blockade, was vital to Union victory.

The great legends of the war center on the land struggles. The ultimate outcome, however, was strongly influenced by strangling the South at sea. If she could not send her cotton and other exports to European markets and bring back the munitions, arms, medical supplies, clothing and other necessities she lacked, her defeat was inevitable. The blockade, gradually mounting in effectiveness from late April, was therefore one of the decisive actions of the conflict. But it did not go unchallenged.

Great Britain did not relish the threat of her looms standing idle because of the loss of her cotton imports from the South. There was good reason for federal shipowners, marine insurers and the Government itself to fear that for a number of reasons England would intervene to aid the Confederacy.

While the fears of direct recognition of the Confederacy as a nation and intervention by Great Britain and others were not realized, there were activities abroad that hindered the North. A few raiders privately built and equipped in Great Britain launched a systematic campaign to drive Union ships off the seas and reopen the lanes to Southern craft. As the war ground on, Union shipowners were justifiably frightened and many of them considered deactivating their vessels. Others later panicked and placed their fleets on the market at give-away prices.

John Divine Jones had foreseen the grim potentialities of the situation. Unless some financial protection could be provided, Union shipping might well be paralyzed while victory on land was in sight.

Jones asked Captain Charles H. Marshall, one of his company's trustees, to accompany him to Washington to confer with Abraham Lincoln. The President was pleased to receive the two visitors from New York. Their mission was constructive, and they provided welcome relief from the politicians and military men who bedeviled him.

The Atlantic men—in contrast to some other marine insurers—were ready to provide protection for federal shipping. But with the welfare of their company and its policyholders in mind, they naturally sought an equitable arrangement to assure them that when hostilities ceased, claims for reimbursement would be made upon England for damage inflicted on Union shipping by cruisers emerging from British ports.

Mr. Lincoln and Secretary of State Seward gave their pledge that such claims would be pressed. They further stressed that as soon as practicable the sea lanes would be patrolled.

Good faith on both sides of a bargain was the operating principle of Atlantic, and the word of Mr. Lincoln was enough for Mr. Jones. He promised to undertake his share of the war risks, shook hands and returned to New York.

Early in the war England had issued the Queen's Proclamation of Neutrality. The Confederacy was recognized as a belligerent, but there was to be no intervention. Despite this reassuring document, shipwrights worked overtime in the yards of Great Britain, building raiders for the Southern cause. Among them were the *Florida, Georgia* and *Alabama*. While some vessels were built for the Confederacy, others were purchased. For example, the renowned *Shenandoah* had been in the East India trade.

The *Alabama* was the most formidable of all the raiders. Her commander was Raphael Semmes of Maryland, a veteran of the U.S. Navy since 1826, who had gone to Richmond early in 1861 and promised Confederate officials: "Give me the right type of ship and I'll do the job." He later got his wish, and he came close to keeping his dire promise.

In a shipyard at Birkenhead, England, work was completed in 1862 on a 1,050-ton raider. She was rigged to carry more than the ordinary spread of canvas, and she had two engines, each producing 300 horsepower. She was an ideal combination of windship and steamship. Her coal bunker would hold enough fuel for eighteen days at sea under maximum steam. Her speed, under any but the most adverse weather conditions, was about 10 knots under steam and 13 knots with sail added—a match for the fastest ship under any flag at that time. This was the *Alabama*. A brief account of her depredations is essential to full understanding of the most important historical episode in which Atlantic has been involved—the *Alabama* Claims.

Alarmed by news of the vessel's completion and its intended use, Charles Francis Adams, U. S. Minister to England, protested to the British government, which issued an order that the *Alabama* was not to sail. But she had already left Birkenhead on the pretext of a trial run. Once out of the harbor, she left a boiling wake as she sped to the Azores to take on guns and stores. She was then entrusted to the command of the eager Semmes. At last, he had the "right" ship. What he did with it is history.

Beginning in September, 1862, Semmes struck terror into Northern shipping circles. In a matter of weeks he sank ten vessels.

Beside himself with worry and fury, U. S. Secretary of the Navy Gideon Welles sent twelve warships on the trail of the *Alabama*. One was the *Kearsarge*, but she was not to keep her fatal date with the raider for almost two years.

Meanwhile, the *Alabama* streaked through the seas over more than two-thirds of the globe. Some sixty-five Union ships fell to her; fifty-five were destroyed; and ten were placed under bond. The *Disaster Books* of Atlantic Mutual reveal that many of these ships were insured by the company.

But in June, 1864, the *Alabama* sailed into Cherbourg for repairs. This was her last harbor. The *Kearsarge,* assigned two years before to track down the *Alabama* and other destroyers of commerce, followed her to the port and trapped her quarry.

Captain Semmes announced his intention of engaging the *Kearsarge*. The word not only reached Captain John A. Winslow, the latter's commander, but it was publicized in the English and French newspapers.

Thus, crowds of spectators gathered along the coasts on the bright Sunday morning of June 19 when the *Alabama* steamed confidently out into the English Channel. The *Kearsarge*, protected by sheet metal chains under her wooden exterior, withstood the *Alabama's* cannonade and soon pierced her at her water line. She turned and tried to make the French coast, but the *Kearsarge* steered across her bow. The *Alabama* struck her flag, lowered boats and sent men to her conqueror to concede surrender and ask for aid, which was forthcoming.

The English yacht *Deerhound,* which had stood by during the engagement, sent boats to pick up Captain Semmes, his officers and a number of his men. They reached safe harbor in England.

The *Alabama* was no more, and the entire North, including the officers of Atlantic and of other insurers, breathed easier. Their relief was premature. They still had to reckon with the *Shenandoah*. She was to cause Atlantic its heaviest losses in connection with the war.

Although the flamboyant Semmes and his *Alabama* became the legendary symbols of the Confederate raiders, the *Shenandoah* took almost as heavy a toll of federal shipping—and in far less time. The *Alabama* was responsible for an estimated $6,547,609 in losses in her twenty-one-month career. The *Shenandoah* came close with $6,487,-000, although she was not commissioned until late in 1864 when the end of the conflict was in sight.

This 790-ton marauder, small by comparison with the *Alabama,* was bought at Glasgow by intermediaries for the Confederacy. Her prospects for a long career did not seem bright. Nevertheless, the *Shenandoah* set her sights on the whaling fleet out of New England and relentlessly pursued this key unit of Northern commerce.

Her captain, James Waddell, was an intrepid and single-minded North Carolinian. Early in April, 1865, he cornered and sank four whalers in the Pacific. Before he sent the vessels to the bottom, Waddell sought and found detailed charts that traced the probable route of the main whaling fleet in the Bering Sea.

On April 13, four days after Lee's surrender, he pointed the *Shenandoah* northward on the charted heels of her prey.

From June 22 through June 28, the *Shenandoah* took twenty-two prizes. The vessels that were spared were used to carry the crews of the sunken ships under bond to San Francisco.

The skipper of the *William Thompson,* one of the vessels taken during that fateful week in June, angrily thrust San Francisco newspaper accounts of Lee's surrender under Captain Wadell's nose. But the master of the *Shenandoah* was hard to convince. What he considered conflicting statements in the newspapers made the whole story suspect in his eyes. Waddell did not accept the truth of the Confederacy's defeat until August, when a British shipmaster confirmed it.

Meanwhile, Waddell stubbornly pushed the *Shenandoah* on in search of still more victims. On June 28—almost three months after Lee's surrender—she won her greatest victory and one of the most remarkable in naval annals. Finding five whalers becalmed and helplessly riding the icy seas, Waddell sent out separate boarding craft and captured them all in one foray. Later that day, he trapped five more ships farther north. All prisoners were placed aboard two of the captured craft. The remaining eight were destroyed. In addition, Waddell took the barque *Waverley* on the same day.

A Confederate observer, awed by the sight of New England's whaling fleet burning through the night amid the Arctic ice crags, wrote: "When—one by one—the burning hulks went hissing and gurgling down into the treacherous bosom of the ocean, the last act in the bloody drama of the American Civil War had been played."

But it was not the last act for Atlantic. An even more fascinating story began after the whalers went down.

The plot of this narrative hinges on the tortoise pace of communications in the 1860s. One fatal example was the delay in the official news of the war's end reaching the daring Waddell. In turn, news of his exploit in destroying the whaling fleet was maddeningly slow in arriving in California.

In July—long after the *Shenandoah*'s work was done—rumors belatedly swept San Francisco that the raider was on her way to hunt down the fleet in the Arctic. Terrified shipowners back in New England heard the gossip late in July and immediately began to seek insurance against the unforeseen menace. They felt that Atlantic would not fail to meet their needs, and they were right.

In just three days, the company, negotiating by telegraph, arranged the desired coverage. Some $350,000 in premiums was involved. In one day, the company received $118,978, its largest payment during a twenty-four-hour period until World War I.

All Atlantic asked of the New England shipowners was a stipulation that no word of the fleet's loss had reached the owners at the time the insurance became effective. This being understood, Atlantic accepted the applications for coverage under an insurance clause containing the wording "lost or not lost." By the terms of this clause, a vessel was insured as of a certain date, even though it later developed that she had actually been lost or damaged before that time.

And so, the whaling fleet was "covered" under Atlantic policies, weeks after many of the ships had found sea bottom. The policies paid off.

But because John Divine Jones had Abraham Lincoln's pledge that if England intervened in the war at sea the Crown would be billed for every federal ship sunk or damaged, the final chapter of Atlantic's leading role in the conflict and her involvement with the raiders has not been written to this day. Unhappily, Lincoln was not alive to fulfill his promise, but the Government lived up to his word—at least in the preliminary stages of attempted recovery from England.

At war's end, the U. S. Government demanded restitution from Great Britain. In the Treaty of Washington, signed in 1871, England agreed that there would be submitted to the International Tribunal of Arbitration at Geneva an itemized and endorsed list of claims growing out of damages inflicted by Confederate raiders. The damages

The Confederate warship *Shenandoah*, prowling the Arctic Ocean in June, 1865, discovered New England's great whaling fleet. Unconvinced that the war was over, the captain sank or captured twenty-five ships in one week. Another month passed before northern shipowners heard that the *Shenandoah* might be headed for the Arctic. They turned to Atlantic Mutual which insured the whalers on a "lost or not lost basis." This meant that the ships were protected even if they were already sunk, as most of them were.

sought were identified as the *Alabama* Claims—in recognition of that vessel's long career in leadership in the destruction of federal shipping.

The international tribunal carefully considered all classes of claims and, in September, 1872, ordered England to pay $12 million in gold, plus $3.5 million in interest. Atlantic's claim of $1,653,000 was the largest among those granted.

In his book *When the Guns Roared,* published in 1965 by Doubleday & Co., Philip Van Doren Stern notes that no actual metal was ever shipped for both countries were afraid that the transfer of 28½ tons of gold might upset the market. On September 9, 1873, a single hand-engrossed certificate for the full amount was presented to the Treasury Department in Washington, thus completing the payment.

The tribunal had explicitly ruled that the money was owed to a group of private and established claimants. The award was to be held in trust for them; it was not to go to anyone else. The U. S. Government was never considered a party to the award nor was Congress.

But when the funds arrived in this country, a group of congressmen had already formed their own ideas of what should be done with the *Alabama* award money. After several debates, Congress agreed to consider who might be the "real claimants." A number of the legislators decided to support "private bills" for anyone who had a claim for damages as a result of the Civil War.

A Massachusetts legislator told Congress: "It is the money of the United States to be disposed of as it pleases, subject to no trust, and especially to no legal right of any individual or corporation." Congress agreed with him.

In the words of one newspaper editor, this action was equivalent to telling the claimants: "We used your paw to snatch the hot chestnut and now we think we will enjoy its flavor while you get treatment for your burns."

Congress informed Atlantic that the company's views were well known, had been completely discussed and would not be officially considered at that time.

Congress then began to prepare a report to guide the decisions of a special compensation committee that eventually was to make the awards. The insurance companies were not permitted to speak for themselves in the legislative deliberations. When attacked, they could not offer direct rebuttal.

Typical of the reports of the discussions was one made by several members of a House subcommittee. This said in part: "What claims have these insurance companies against Congress? They have none whatsoever in law or equity; the country is under no obligation to them; they assumed war risks voluntarily."

Congress finally decided to introduce legislation which would recognize the suffering of the country as a whole and which would provide that the newly appointed *Alabama* Claims Commissioners allocate the funds "in the best interests of the nation." This legislation meant a complete refusal to pay the insurance companies, as directed by the tribunal, since it would delegate to the commissioners the responsibility of meeting national interests rather than individual claims. "National interests" was a rather flexible term.

One New England senator did not feel that England would ever have paid the money if it had thought that the insurance companies would get any of it before all other war sufferers were compensated. Yet the tribunal had specifically made the award to the insurers, and Great Britain had paid its bill primarily on the evidence they produced.

A Senate bill was finally reported out of committee and, if anything, was made more unjust by floor amendments. The House followed the Senate's track in setting up the awards commission but went even further. It produced a measure that totally ignored the treaty and sanctioned payments to some shipowners who had carried no insurance and had lost no vessels.

Under congressional direction, the *Alabama* Claims Commissioners then went to work and distributed approximately $10 million. The commissioners did not stop at paying off uninsured shipowners and merchants. They reimbursed those who had lost money while pursuing normal commerce; they dispensed funds to those specifically excluded by the tribunal; they rewarded opportunists; and they paid those who, in the opinion of Congress, "deserved" payment. They paid everyone in sight—except the deserving—and when the distribution had been completed, they had $5.5 million left. But there was not one penny for insurance companies.

Congress and President Grant congratulated each other and the commissioners on their success in dispensing the claims money. Even *The New York Times* felt at first that Grant and Congress deserved a tribute for carrying on their labors with diligence and general satisfaction.

The insurance companies ruefully conceded that diligence had been applied; but it was mainly in the successful effort to twist the intent of the tribunal and to exclude them unjustly.

The *Times* finally noted that possibly the commission had been a little too liberal and also that it had handed out money to some who perhaps were not entitled to it.

Clifford A. Hand, a lawyer of renown and an Atlantic trustee from 1859 to 1901, was retained to present the company's case to Congress. This distinguished attorney, the uncle of the famous Learned Hand, who later graced the U. S. circuit court for many years, was to continue until 1882 his determined efforts to secure fair treatment from Congress. But that body remained deaf even to his eloquent pleas.

At the end of 1881, the *Daily Commercial Bulletin of New York* printed its last comment on the subject: "The money was received in payment of an itemized bill. It is for Congress to relieve the nation of what bids to become a disgrace and national scandal." Even this barb was not sharp enough to pierce congressional hides. And so the case was closed.

A mathematically inclined staff member of Atlantic has computed the interest on its unpaid award of $1,653,000 at $393,736,000 as of December 31, 1966. The company has long since ceased to press its well-grounded case, although in the past the officials have often wondered what would have happened if the situation had been reversed and the Government were awaiting payment.

But this speculation was idle. Unfortunately, so too was the company's long-cherished hope that it might one day receive the funds for the benefit of its policyholders. And yet, that would have been no more than a fitting tribute to two men who made a pact in good faith —Abraham Lincoln and John Divine Jones.

In addition to its underwriting support of national interests during the war, Atlantic aided the government of its home state by substantial investments to help provide funds for emergencies.

For example, in 1864, the company subscribed for $100,000 of riot damage bonds issued by New York County. These securities were unique in American history.

In August, 1862, President Lincoln had called for 300,000 men to serve in the army for nine months. If the quota was not filled, the President warned, it would be necessary to resort to a draft. Secretary of War Stanton put the draft into effect but had to withdraw the order when riots broke out in Wisconsin and Indiana, and the opposition of governors bolstered the resistance. These were but mild harbingers of further trouble to come.

The Government passed the enrollment act in March of 1863. After the names of draftees were published, a mob of 50,000 surged through the streets of New York City from July 13 to July 16, setting fires and otherwise terrorizing the populace. A church and an orphanage were burned. The rioters invaded the offices of the *New York Tribune* and caused heavy destruction. Before their fury was spent, twelve persons had been killed and innumerable others severely injured. More than $1.5 million in damaged property lay in the mob's wake. The insurrection ended when troops from the Army of the Potomac marched into New York and killed or wounded more than 1,000 of the rioters. To pay for the havoc, New York County floated the riot damage bonds, and Atlantic was among the early subscribers.

The company also bought $100,000 New York County's Soldier Bounty Fund Bonds just before the surrender at Appomattox in April, 1865. This was also an unusual type of security. To stimulate northern enlistments, bounties had been paid by federal, state and local authorities. Congress sanctioned payments of $100 to those enlisting for three years. After the enrollment act of 1863, which set off the New York draft riots, bounties were raised, some getting $100, others as much as $400.

The states paid bounties in order to fill the ranks without conscription, which was considered a disgrace to any congressional district having to resort to it. The result was that wealthy districts lured men away from poorer sections with the promise of a high bounty.

Unscrupulous bounty brokers and agents recruited men, collected the fees and then gave their clients a modest portion of it or none at all. Bounty jumpers—with the aid of crooked brokers and agents—

would enlist in one locality, collect their payments, desert, reenlist in another district and repeat the performance until they tired of it or were apprehended. One "volunteer" deserted thirty-two times.

The generous payments, coupled with loose administration of the system, brought total bounties for the war to the staggering sum of $750 million. In the last two years of the struggle, the states and local authorities paid out about $300 million. To help restore its treasury, New York County issued bounty bonds and found a ready buyer in Atlantic.

A Half Century of Progress

When a company enjoys almost uninterrupted success in its early years, as Atlantic did, its leaders inevitably emerge as the unreal and perfect cardboard figures so typical of the "founding fathers" in most business histories. But with all their merits, neither Walter Restored Jones nor John Divine Jones was a paragon. Both tended to carry their virtues to excess.

The first president was a man of driving energy and determination. He was incapable of satisfaction with any personal achievement that fell short of perfection. While laudable, such standards are generally beyond human reach, and Jones's inability to accept poor company results even for the one year of 1854 and his apparent assumption of the blame for the downturn contributed directly to his death and to the consequent loss of his counsel to the company.

John D. Jones was a more complex individual than his uncle.

Despite a serene and almost benign appearance and manner, he was not to be trifled with nor intimidated. He proved this many times, notably when he got word early in his presidency that Atlantic was committed for more than $600,000 on a big tea clipper out of Hong Kong for San Francisco.

Jones went into the market to find other companies to share the risk by reinsuring Atlantic. Today, that reinsurance would be virtually automatic. But in the last century such facilities were neither numerous nor readily accessible. Moreover, the market quickly concluded that Jones was in a predicament. Not without relish, the potential reinsurers, thinking they had him in a corner, asked for an unfairly high rate to assume part of the risk. Jones promptly told them to go to perdition and decided that Atlantic would carry the entire line. Fortunately, the tea clipper came through without incident, but Jones's decision to bear the entire risk was a hard one. More than a century later, Miles F. York, tenth president of the company, said it took more nerve than modern management would be able to muster.

Jones's firmness as an administrator was illustrated early in his presidency when he put into effect "Regulations for the Government of the Clerks of the Atlantic Mutual Insurance Company." This document—by today's standards—painted a rather dismal picture of an employee's workday:

"Clerks must be at their desks to commence business, between April 1 and September 30, not later than 8:30 A.M. Between Oct. 1 and March 31, not later than 9 A.M.

"They must not leave the office before 6 P.M. and not then, unless the work in their respective departments is completed.

"They must not leave their desks temporarily during the day without leaving a substitute to answer for them.

"They must not absent themselves from the office (except in case of illness) without permission of the President or Vice President being first obtained.

"No loud talking, laughing or gossiping will be permitted.

"Smoking, or the lighting of segars [*sic*] or pipes in the office at any or all times is strictly prohibited.

"Each person, upon leaving his desk at the close of business for the day, must see that the gas at his desk is turned off, and will be held responsible therefor."

Jones's determination, self-sufficiency and, above all, his durability proved to be mixed blessings for the future of the company.

In his memoirs, William D. Winter attributed many of the company's "gray days" to the dead hand of aged administrators. Their accession to high office through the years became inevitable during the term of John D. Jones.

In modern times, ten years is a reasonably long tenure for a corporation president. But after a full decade as the head of Atlantic, Jones was just getting his second wind. In 1865 he was only fifty-one years of age and at the peak of his powers. With today's pension and retirement provisions he would have relinquished office at age sixty-five in 1879. But the resolute Jones held his grip on the presidency until 1895 when he was eighty-one. Thus a lid was clamped on the fortunes and advancement of others who might have more vigorously led the enterprise had they been given the opportunity earlier in their careers.

Serving under Jones were three men who later became presidents of the company. William H. H. Moore was head of the loss department. He had a long and distinguished career behind him when on Jones's death he was named president at seventy-one. By then he was understandably averse to new adventures, and after a year and a half he turned the post over with relief to Anton A. Raven, who was sixty-four. Raven clung to the presidency until he was eighty-two, when he was succeeded in 1915 by the sixty-six-year-old Cornelius Eldert. Eldert, who had joined the company in 1865, continued as president until he was eighty-one in 1930. His career is particularly remarkable since it spanned the fateful years of change between the close of the Civil War and the great depression of the 1930s. In effect, both he and Raven were men trained in 19th century precepts, trying to apply them to the problems of the 20th century.

With three men successively assuming leadership at ages that would qualify them for retirement today, lack of sustained growth for Atlantic was inevitable. This is not to imply that the trio did not make contributions to the company. Moore and Eldert administered its affairs prudently and maintained its high operating principles. But

In 1871, thirty-three intrepid whaling captains took their ships north of Alaska. Leading into rich whaling fields was a clear strip of water between jaws of treacherous ice. The fleet went in; but the wind shifted and all thirty-three vessels were crushed in the grinding ice. Most of the fleet hailed from New Bedford and sailed under insurance coverage written by four prominent marine insurers of the day. Only one—Atlantic—survives.

they were innately conservators. Raven was an aggressive leader for a good part of his term, but he unwisely remained until his once formidable powers had waned.

The consequences of unprogressive management took some time in coming; when they did, the cost to Atlantic was heavy.

The results of another managerial transgression—not so serious as the problem of outmoded administration, but undesirable nevertheless—appeared during the presidency of John D. Jones. He and his uncle shared a predilection for hiring relatives. Frank D. Denton, who later became secretary of the company, noted this weakness when he started his career with Atlantic in 1889. In his salty recollections, *49 Years at 49 Wall Street,* he comments on the nepotism of John D. Jones: "During his regime, any Joneses not dead and reposing in the Jones Memorial Cemetery at Cold Spring Harbor, Long Island, could be found on the payroll."

Denton documented his observation by listing the roster of employees, on which he was designated "Boy." Of sixty-five members of Atlantic's staff, thirteen were in some way related to the Jones family. This figure did not include President Jones himself nor Mr. Moore, who was also a "connection." Thus, fifteen of the sixty-five persons on Atlantic's staff had family ties, a circumstance that must have been discouraging for the other fifty when it was time for a pay raise or a promotion.

The building janitor, three watchmen and three waiters in the company dining room rounded out the roster, but they were beyond suspicion since relatives were interested only in more exalted stations.

But nepotism or not and in spite of the *Alabama* Claims and other problems posed by the Civil War, John D. Jones had no need to apologize for his conduct of the company during the struggle and in the crucial afteryears. At war's beginning in 1861, Atlantic was writing $3.6 million in premiums. The figure rose to a new high of $6,886,721 in 1864, and the company paid a 40% dividend. In the first year of peace, premiums remained high at $5,920,507.

Being a realist, Jones would have been the first to acknowledge that Atlantic's continuing success from 1865 to 1894, the year before he died, was based primarily on the unprecedented growth of the country. Nevertheless, the president's challenging task was to get a desired share of profitable business in the face of foreign insurance competition attracted by the country's flourishing economy.

In 1869, the Central Pacific Railroad and the Union Pacific were joined at Promontory Point, Utah. When the golden spike was driven to unite the two lines, the continent was linked by steel rails from coast to coast. Part of the agitation for the transcontinental road to the Pacific was due to the sinking in 1857 of the *Central America*—one of Atlantic's risks. This tragedy, described in Chapter Four, helped to spur the advocates of a countrywide railroad to greater efforts. The ill-fated ship had been bound for New York, carrying gold miners on the last leg of the tedious trip from San Francisco, where they had embarked on another steamer and sailed down the lower coast of California to the Isthmus of Panama. Then they crossed by rail to Aspinwall, now Colon, terminal port of the Caribbean. There the *Central America* waited to take them to Havana and then to New York. The entire trip took five to six weeks, and the toll of shipping on the dangerous route, climaxed by the *Central America*'s loss, was severe. Hence the clamor for a transcontinental road, which would be speedier and safer and would permit transportation of infinitely more goods from coast to coast and across worldwide waters, grew until its proponents were successful.

In addition to its role as underwriter of the ship whose sinking gave the advocates of the coast-to-coast railroad one of their strongest talking points, Atlantic played a much more direct and important role in the realization of the transcontinental line. Beginning in 1866, the company made heavy investments in the bonds of the Union Pacific Railroad Co. The initial purchase was $250,000 of these securities. For the next decade, while Union Pacific was engaged in building and then in establishing the success of the new system, Atlantic made additional and substantial purchases of its bonds.

Support was also given to the partner in linking the continent—Central Pacific Railroad. Atlantic bought $50,000 of its bonds in 1868 and continued to add to its investment during the vitally important years of early operation from one end of the country to the other.

In the same period, many other new railroads crisscrossed the country to accommodate the booming commerce. Industry, which had been secondary to agriculture before the Civil War, began to predominate. By the 1880s the value of American manufactured goods surpassed that of farm products for the first time. In 1894, the country became the leading manufacturing nation of the world.

Other developments significant to Atlantic marked the 1870s. Refrigerated railroad cars and ships made possible delivery of many types of food to faraway ports. Gustavus Swift began shipping refrigerated dressed beef from Chicago to both coasts for domestic and later for foreign sale. Commercial canning got under way on a big scale. H. J. Heinz put out the first of his 57 varieties for world trade.

By 1870 the population of the country had more than doubled—since 1842—from slightly more than 18 million to almost 40 million.

All of these developments would seemingly have guaranteed Atlantic's automatic progress. But there was a less rosy side to the picture: Competition from abroad was attracted by American prosperity. The base for this competition had been established by the British before the Civil War. Determined to end the sway of the American clippers, Great Britain began to build steamships. As Winter notes in his *Marine Insurance*, the glory of the clippers began to fade. Slow in developing her resources of iron and coal, the United States began to wane as an overseas carrying nation. By the time American shipbuilders realized that iron and coal were to control world commerce, the nation was involved in the Civil War. This hastened the decline of the American merchant marine and led to the financial embarrassment of most U. S. marine insurers and to the failure of many. Because of heavy taxation and the loss of profitable overseas traffic in many products, particularly cotton, American shipping and its allied interests were partially crippled.

Seizing its opportunity, Great Britain entered a new era of shipbuilding and maritime operation. Her new metal vessels with mechanical power soon took over much of the foreign trade of the United States.

In the postwar years, the situation was intensified. Shortsighted legislation permitted the entrance into the American market of foreign insurers on terms which militated against the native companies. The first British company was admitted in 1871 and was quickly followed by many others. These firms had been in business many years. They were skillfully managed and had larger surpluses than American insurers. They were able to cut rates in a frenzied drive for business.

The domestic companies, unprepared to meet this sort of competition, were gradually forced out of the marine field. Some were liquidated. Others that did both a fire and marine business were happy to concentrate on fire.

The American market still controlled a respectable amount of cargo business, but the British had all but preempted the hull line. Moreover, they dictated the forms and the terms on which hull business was to be written.

This was the competitive climate John D. Jones faced as a challenge. How well he met it is a matter of record. In 1873—a year in which the struggle for business was at its height—Atlantic declared a 50% dividend. Moreover, the volume of business remained so high that for the first time full underwriting powers were delegated to several employees. One was Raven, who had long conducted the company's correspondence and then had become an assistant underwriter with limited authority to exercise judgment.

Jones had decided that the company needed all the underwriting talent it could muster. Not only did the growing volume and variety of risks pose a severe challenge to those making the decisions on the business Atlantic should accept but some shippers were resorting to shady practices.

Their ingenuity is illustrated in an incident described in Atlantic's *Disaster Books* for 1870. Early in the year, the steamship *George Washington* left New York for New Orleans. Atlantic had $83,400 at risk on the hull and the cargo.

Fire broke out below decks a few days after she left port. The captain traced the source of the smoke to a lower hold where he found a smoldering 4-foot-square box. This was marked "Handle with Care—Keep Dry." Its owners had claimed that the box contained valuable machinery.

The captain soon found that the contents could loosely have been labeled machinery, but it was of the type to be made famous many years later by Rube Goldberg. It consisted of a 1-gallon can of spirits of turpentine, a soda-water bottle filled with gasoline, two cigar boxes in which nestled several families of white mice, a highly explosive compound of potassium chloride, and packing of straw and sawdust.

The bizarre content was arranged in such a way that the mice would nibble at one of the containers and set off the explosive. This in turn would ignite the turpentine, gasoline, straw and sawdust. The fire would then gain headway in the lower hold and would wipe out ship, cargo and crew, destroying all evidence in the process. Thus the incendiary box—worth about $10—would return many times its value to the shippers, including $83,400 from Atlantic. Thanks to a vigilant captain and crew, the ingenious plan failed.

A famous attempt at fraud was perpetrated by a French resident of New York who chartered a Maine brig, put his own captain aboard and sent her to Havre. The captain purchased valuable silks at Paris and received the necessary inspection marks from the customs authorities there, making further examination at Havre unnecessary. Before that port was reached, the silks were removed and rubbish was substituted for them. When the brig was well at sea, holes were bored in the hull, but a zealous mate—not in on the conspiracy—plugged them up. More holes were bored when he was off watch, and the crew abandoned the sinking brig. But the expected insurance payment on the "missing" silks was not made. A French captain in New York who had been cautiously approached about assuming command had indignantly refused and had communicated his suspicions to the president of an insurer. The merchant was tried for fraud, and the ship's captain was charged with the more serious crime of barratry for sinking his vessel.

Such episodes continued through the years and were disturbing to Jones, especially when Atlantic was involved. One of the reasons he bolstered his underwriting staff was his unwillingness to rely on captains and crews to foil plots against Atlantic. That was no way to run the company. A better way was dependence on his own underwriters to appraise the moral character of shippers before their vessels left port. This was a task at which the shrewd Raven excelled for many years.

The shape of things to come in the insurance business had been foreshadowed in 1864 when the first casualty policy was written in the United States by the newly formed Travelers Insurance Company. This policy was for accident coverage and, as the company's name implied, protected travelers. It was not long, however, before the company was writing both accident and life insurance on others.

Shortly thereafter, Travelers began issuing liability coverage. The first form it sold was employers' liability for accidents to employees of business enterprises. This was the forerunner of workmen's compensation.

Fully occupied with its own problems—limited to the marine field—Atlantic was not immediately concerned with these new casualty developments. Nor was it concerned with fire insurance, which had been well established in the United States since the 1700s, although the original charter permitted Atlantic to write that type of business.

John D. Jones and his colleagues must have been thankful they had no fire insurance interests in 1871 when Chicago, the fastest-growing city in the United States, went up in flames.

The city's structures had been thrown up in haste and made of inferior materials. Only about a third were of masonry, and many of these had wooden shingles. Chicago was a network of firetraps with only volunteer firemen to protect it from disaster.

Local fire insurance companies were growing at the same rate as the city. They had little or nothing in surplus and reserves, and few of the officials knew or cared about any aspect of the business, except selling policies.

On October 8, 1871, fire broke out on the west side of Chicago. Fanned by a strong wind and feeding on dry wood after fourteen weeks of drought, the conflagration raged for close to 30 hours until it partially burned itself out. A providential rain finally extinguished the fire completely.

An area of 5 square miles had been destroyed. About 90,000 were homeless. Some 250 were dead. Every building of any consequence had been burned. Property valued at $200 million was wiped out. Less than half of that was insured. Of some 250 insurers, about 70 went out of business immediately. Only a few losses were paid in full, with some payments as low as three to eight cents on the dollar. Of $88 million in estimated losses, only $45 to $50 million was paid.

Just thirteen months later, after a holocaust in Boston, thirty more fire companies went bankrupt, their total losses being double their assets.

Although Atlantic had no interest in the new casualty business of that era and fortunately was not active in fire insurance, many years later, William D. Winter, the company's most aggressive president, played a leading role in making it possible for his company and all insurers to write these and other lines of business under multiple line charter powers.

But his progressive leadership still lay some seventy years ahead. Meanwhile, the procession that was to bring older men to the management of Atlantic seemed to move by destiny. Raven became fourth vice-president in 1874, advanced to the third rank in 1876 and in the next decade moved in behind Moore, who became first vice-president in 1887 when he was sixty-three.

In those smooth years of profitable operation, the problem of presidential succession did not overly concern the trustees. They were taking great satisfaction in results, particularly in a statement prepared for the annual meeting of January, 1890, which traced the company's cumulative performance from its founding in April, 1842. This showed that it had written premiums of $176,452,538.41. It had paid losses of $103,255,352.05. The tremendous sum paid for redemption of scrip was $55,168,610. Interest on these came to $12,778,024.65. Certificates still outstanding were worth $6,888,640.

On the basis of these outstanding achievements, the trustees retained their confidence in John D. Jones. In the company's 50th anniversary year of 1892, he had been president thirty-seven years. Although he was more and more frequently absent from the office, according to the sharp-eyed office boy Frank Denton, he held the reins of management firmly, and his appearance at his desk always created a flutter from the first vice-president to the clerks. He had no compunction about reversing a decision of any executive officer. This was not done unpleasantly but more in the manner of a fond parent setting the house to rights after an absence. He was apt to call for any book of record, and the keeper of that tome sighed with relief when it was returned without comment.

Jones abhorred nonsense, even when it appeared in the form of a compliment directed to him. Thus, when, early in 1892, the trustees felicitated him for the uniformly good results he had achieved and for having reduced insurance to a science, he promptly dispelled that notion. He told the trustees that the business was anything but a science. He pointed out that the company's success was due to hard work and incessant watchfulness on the part of all hands. Present Atlantic management agrees with him.

Jones died in 1895 at his country home in Massapequa, Long Island. His body was brought from there on the Long Island Railroad to Brooklyn, across on the Wall Street ferry and through the length of Wall Street, past the offices of the company that he had served almost all his business life, to Trinity Church. When the cortege reached the corner of Wall and William streets, nearly the whole office force joined the procession and escorted the former chief through the gates of Old Trinity. As the cortege passed the Subtreasury, the national flag on that building was lowered until the procession passed. This was done by order of the Secretary of the Treasury.

Moore was elevated to president. He had long dreaded the prospect and had confided this to his colleague Raven, who held exactly opposite views of the job. He could scarcely wait to take the presidential chair.

The ascetic and gentlemanly Moore, another Long Islander, was a graduate of Union College, New York. He had been with Atlantic since 1855 and was happy in his technical role as an expert adjuster of losses. He had no appetite for larger administrative problems, and after eighteen uneasy months in the presidential post he more than willingly turned it over to the eager Raven. Moore remained as an advisory member of the finance committee. Atlantic began another era under the tempestuous Raven.

New Era; Old Leaders

On a visit to Atlantic's offices in the fall of 1964 to attend a trustees' meeting, J. Arthur Bogardus, president of the company from 1946 to 1951, was delighted to be asked for a firsthand description of Raven.

"When I joined the company in 1904 as office boy," Mr. Bogardus said, "Raven had been President for seven years. He was then seventy-one years old, but he could move faster than any man in my recollection. He seemed to skim over the ground. When we boys were up to some prank, we'd look around to make sure the President was at the other end of the office. Even then, we were often startled to find him glowering right behind us before our little joke was finished."

Mr. Bogardus recalled Raven as a stocky figure below medium height. An immense domed head—size 7¾ and devoid of hair—seemed to make up for the stature he lacked in leg and trunk. Owlish eyes behind steel-rimmed glasses and a tiny goatee beneath his compressed mouth gave him a no-nonsense look, which was anything but misleading.

This doughty little Dutchman was born in Curaçao. A mixture of highly contradictory characteristics, he was domineering yet kindly; courageous but cautious. Often guilty of a complete lack of tact in dealing with subordinates on business matters, he was at the same time a soft touch for any charitable appeal that reached his sensibilities. Nor would he tolerate discrimination against anyone because of supposedly inferior station. Raven reserved his most violent dislike for the British because they opposed his countrymen in the Boer War.

With this complex character in command, the officers and staff of Atlantic anticipated an explosive atmosphere, and their apprehensions were justified.

Fittingly enough, the first significant national event of his term in office was the blowing up of the *Maine* in Havana Harbor and the start of the Spanish-American War. Once again, Atlantic was called upon for war-risk protection. The company came through with comparatively small losses.

At the end of the war and in the ensuing years, Raven found himself the head of a company whose horizons were immeasurably broadened along with those of the country itself. The economic climate was ideal for company growth. The United States had assumed a protectorate over Cuba and had acquired Puerto Rico, Guam and the Philippines.

This meant still more new markets for U. S. products. Commercial and political isolation belonged to the past. The country began to take its place in international affairs and to share the responsibilities of leadership.

In spite of his idiosyncrasies, Raven was an underwriter of acumen and skill in his early years as president. When he took the leading line on a risk, the rest of the market followed with confidence. After all, he had served under both Walter R. Jones and John D. Jones and had absorbed their precepts. However, this experience, which was of benefit on the one hand, may have been harmful on the other. It was rooted in outmoded ideas of individual performance. When Raven took over, he faced a new age with vastly different problems. No one man could cope with them. Yet Raven had not been trained to share responsibilities with his associates. They were not permitted to gain overall knowledge of the conduct of the business.

The same secrecy pervaded the entire company. Each department head believed that he was the keeper of some particular phase of the operation, and each saw to it that no one shared his special knowledge. Accordingly, when a senior was removed by death or otherwise, his junior had to dig painstakingly through the books to learn the secrets of how particular departmental functions were conducted. From the top down, management was unwilling to share authority with juniors. Any effort on their part to make decisions, even in minor matters, was frowned upon.

This regrettable tendency was illustrated by an incident involving two of the most vivid personalities in Atlantic's history: Raven and Winter, a man whose Scotch stubbornness fully matched Raven's Dutch obstinacy. These two Atlantic immortals clashed head-on many times, and sparks invariably flew. This is all the more remarkable because Winter as a boy was a member of Raven's church in Brooklyn and got his first job in 1901 through the peppery Dutchman. At first the latter was solicitous of his recruit's welfare, but this attitude soon changed as the youth demonstrated his aggressiveness.

Matters came to a head in 1902 when the seventeen-year-old Winter, with the company less than a year, decided that a lengthy list of policies he was charged with preparing weekly represented duplicate effort. He showed his immediate superior that the information was already available elsewhere. This gentleman, in keeping with the rest of the staff, had no authority to make decisions. But he was impressed by young Winter's observation, and he proceeded up the aisle to approach the "throne," as Raven's perch was irreverently called by the staff. The supervisor came back rapidly, with flushed face and rising anger. He asked Winter if he knew what the "old man" had said. Obviously the office boy destined to be president did not, and he said so.

"Mr. Raven said to tell that young man he is not paid to think," the supervisor reported. In his reminiscences, Winter wryly notes: "I pondered that thought and reached the conclusion that Raven was very right; at $29.16 a month, one was not paid to think."

But Winter's tenacity would not permit him to drop the matter. He brought it up again three years later. Raven was then more receptive, and the unnecessary work on the list was eliminated. This was one of the few episodes involving these two strong personalities that ended happily.

Raven had made up his mind that Winter would not achieve prominence while he was in control. In one of his typically explosive moments he declared: "If he ever becomes president, that young man will wreck the company." That statement, curiously, illustrates that Raven was both a good and a bad prophet. He was perceptive enough to foresee that Winter might well rise to the top; the rest of the prophecy was fortunately far off the mark. Winter was the man destined to take Atlantic out of the doldrums. Nevertheless he had to wait until Raven was out of office to gain full recognition.

Raven did not confine his personality quirks to the office. He was an ardent foe of tobacco, and he was undoubtedly outraged early in 1900 when the newspapers reported that cigarette consumption in the United States had hit 2.6 billion annually. The president must have taken this news as a personal affront and as evidence that the campaign he had been waging to discourage the use of cigarettes was a failure. He had "No Smoking" signs plastered all over Atlantic's offices and in the elevators, public halls and other rooms of the building. He lectured new employees on the evils of nicotine and told them the majority of inmates of asylums for the feeble-minded were there because of excessive cigarette puffing.

His antipathy extended to cigars and pipes. He did not hesitate to tap strangers on the shoulder in the elevators and corridors of the building, with the curt request that they immediately extinguish whatever form of tobacco they were enjoying. This custom did not endear him to the tenants or to visitors.

Raven soon was enforcing his "No Smoking" rules on a much broader scale, for the company decided in 1900 to erect a new and larger building to replace the old 1851 structure. Raven brought his prohibitive signs along to the new headquarters. Despite the humorous aspects of his one-man campaign against tobacco, Raven's prescience is impressive in the light of modern medical opinion.

The building project was necessary not only because Atlantic needed more modern and expanded offices but because rentals from the old five-story structure did not return revenue in keeping with the choice location at Wall and William streets.

At this juncture, as in the past, Atlantic enjoyed the advantage of a distinguished board of trustees. They enthusiastically supported the new building venture.

Most prominent of the group was Levi P. Morton, a banker who had formed in 1869 the firm of Morton, Bliss & Co. He was elected to Congress in 1878 and 1880 and in 1881 was named Minister to France by President Garfield. While there, he drove the first rivet in the Statue of Liberty, and on July 4, 1884, he accepted from France on behalf of his country the completed statue. He was elected Vice-President of the United States in 1888 and governor of New York in 1894.

One of his colleagues on Atlantic's board was Clement A. Griscom, a Philadelphian. By the time he was thirty, he was vice-president of the International Navigation Co. and later became president. His chief ambition was to expand transatlantic travel, which he did by increasing the safety and comfort of his passengers with such improvements as the transverse bulkhead, watertight compartments and staterooms in suites. International Navigation bought out the American and Inman lines and was renamed the Red Star Line. Later the new company was merged with J. P. Morgan's holdings to form the International Mercantile Marine Co., bringing under one ownership five transatlantic lines with 136 vessels of more than 1 million tons total burden.

Another vital figure on the board as Atlantic entered a new century was Gustav H. Schwab, son of German immigrant parents, who joined the New York office of North German Lloyd Lines as a young man and within twenty years was in complete charge of all its American interests. He was a political reformer and helped to clean up abuses in New York City through revision of ballot and election laws.

These distinguished trustees were joined in the early 1900s by Morris K. Jesup of Westport, Connecticut. After a successful career in railroading, he went into banking and acquired another fortune. He retired from active business at fifty-four, became president of the New York State Chamber of Commerce and devoted himself to philanthropy. He was an incorporator of the American Museum of Natural History in New York City in 1868, gave that organization $2 million and was its president from 1881 to 1908. He was also a financial backer of the Peary expedition to the North Pole and was head of the Peary Arctic Club.

The new eighteen-story Atlantic Building—Wall Street's first skyscraper—was completed on the old site in 1901. It immediately became known as the Building of the Ships. The top four stories of white terra cotta were appropriately embellished with rows of galley prows. From the roof and the higher stories of the building, all of the waterway approaches to New York, with their teeming maritime traffic, could be seen. The *Brooklyn Eagle* described the new skyscraper as "the finest business structure in all its appointments in this country."

Although it now had one of the most up-to-date offices in New York, Atlantic was slow to adopt the modern equipment and changing business practices that marked the turn of the century. For years the management had resisted the use of telephones. Important affairs were transacted in face-to-face meetings. Correspondence was handled by a corps of bearded clerks, chosen for their copperplate handwriting.

Finally, Raven agreed to the installation of a single telephone in a small private booth on the first floor. After this revolutionary concession to progress, Raven issued one of the oddest regulations in the history of American business. He ruled that the new instrument was to be used only for emergency personal calls. No business was to be transacted over the phone; anyone caught using it for that purpose was subject to severe censure and perhaps dismissal. It was not considered safe to entrust Atlantic secrets to the telephone wires that cobwebbed the city in that day.

A junior clerk whose desk was near the booth was assigned to answer all calls and to summon those wanted. No number was listed in the New York telephone directory nor did one appear there in Atlantic's name for some years. Today, at the New York headquarters alone, close to 1 million calls are made and received annually. Contrary to Raven's order, personal calls are not given preference.

The addition of the instrument in 1901 was a major breakthrough. This was followed by another innovation, equally important, and highly appropriate in connection with the telephone: The first woman was added to the staff.

For years, Raven had used a male secretary to take his dictation and to transcribe his letters in longhand. This young man, Robert Montgomery, must have been a student of trends. Early in the 1900s he surveyed the field and decided that the feminine invasion of almost every office in New York doomed his future prospects. He accordingly asked for a transfer to a regular department and was accommodated.

Miss Dorothy Gottschalk thereupon became Atlantic's pioneer female employee as secretary and typist to President Raven. A typewriter was purchased for her, and she took on her formidable assignment and met it with aplomb. She was a considerable attraction and the recipient of overwhelming attention. Atlantic's ladies today are equally deserving of admiration. But in the company's 125th year, there are 600 of them lending charm, devotion and efficiency to the operation. They are under somewhat of a handicap compared with the unique Miss Gottschalk.

When she joined Atlantic, one of the leading figures in the comic strips was a blond beauty known as "Fluffy Ruffles." Miss Gottschalk was a blond; her rebaptism was inevitable.

She soon enjoyed the company of a number of other young women who were added to the staff very gradually. Charles E. Fay, secretary of the company, appointed himself censor of the conversational environment in which the girls operated, and, thanks to his efforts, their sensibilities were spared undue shocks from the language of their male colleagues.

The adoption by so conservative a company as Atlantic of some new methods and practices at the turn of the century gives some indication of the changes that were taking place in American business and social life. But it is necessary to take a broader look at the country in that era to realize that between the founding of Atlantic in 1842 and the year 1900, the United States had been transformed.

There was a vast growth in steel production, resulting from the Bessemer process, the development of the open-hearth furnace and the consequent multiplication of mills. This meant more and better steel for rails, wires, bridges, ships, steel skeleton buildings and a host of other uses. Steel was the basic material of the new industrial age.

Homes, as well as streets, were illuminated by gaslight and then by the magic of electricity. Transportation was magnified with the coming of the cable car, the trolley car, the elevated railroad and then the subway. Railroads had been in their infancy in 1842 but had reached great heights by 1900, as had the steamship.

Then came the prime revolutionizer: The automobile. It had been introduced as early as 1884 but did not begin to take American forms until the 1890s.

The rickety airplane of the Wright brothers skittered along the sands of Kitty Hawk, North Carolina, in 1903, and rose in man's first powered flights. These lasted from 12 seconds to a minute against a strong wind and covered only 120 feet to 582 feet. Nevertheless, when the 200-pound craft took to the air, the jet and space age was foreshadowed.

All these wonders and more introduced a new world that would scarcely have been recognized by Atlantic's founders.

But new world or not and despite its surprising agreement to innovation in several important phases of company activity, Atlantic management resisted change in basic operations in the early 1900s.

Bogardus, who was a minor but exceedingly observant member of the staff in those days, comments on this situation in his memoirs:

"It is difficult to understand why in those years, when our economy was expanding rapidly and marine insurance was being called on for broader and more flexible forms of coverage, we insisted on doing business in the way it had been done since the company was founded. We would not voluntarily issue contract policies covering export shipments and, as a result, not only failed to gain our share of new business but lost some of the best cargo accounts on our books.

"When I first came with the company, we insured many of the national name organizations but they gradually left us. Other companies were issuing contract policies to exporters, giving coverage against theft and pilferage, and extending policies to insure on shore from warehouse to warehouse, while we refused to extend our policies, although frequently paying claims for theft and pilferage and other losses not covered by the policies.

"It is difficult to rationalize the attitude of the company at that

The *Mary Celeste* cleared New York harbor in November of 1872. Her destination was Genoa, Italy. About a month after her departure she was sighted in mid-Atlantic, sailing ghost-like out of the mist. When she was hailed, no one answered. When she was boarded, not a person was found. No one has ever solved the mystery of how the ten passengers and crew of the *Mary Celeste* vanished without a trace. Of all the historic vessels Atlantic Mutual has insured, none has stimulated greater speculation.

time. Possibly it was because so many mutual marine companies had failed and we were the only survivors. This may have led the powers in charge to feel that our method of doing business was the only safe one. The advanced age of those who headed the company may well have been a contributing cause."

Bogardus thus came to the same conclusion as his colleague Winter in analyzing the cause of company stagnation, although he described it more mildly than did Winter in his characteristically pungent phrase: "The dead hand of aged administrators."

Even as young clerks, these two future presidents were in complete agreement that Atlantic should have been progressing with the times. Years later they made sure that it did.

The spring of 1906 brought the worst disaster in insurance history to that time. Shortly past 5 A.M. on April 18, the city of San Francisco shuddered convulsively as the earth's crust parted. The shock was felt from Los Angeles to Coos Bay, Oregon, a distance of more than 700 miles. To the east, the tremor shook communities as far away as 300 miles.

But the city by the Golden Gate bore the brunt of the upheaval. In a little more than 3 hours, more than fifty separate fires raged and then merged as firemen stood helplessly by. The water mains had been cracked and uprooted. For three days and two nights the conflagration continued until the U. S. Army dynamited extensive areas that the fire could not leap. But in its wake lay more than 28,000 buildings and a devastated section of 497 city blocks. Some 452 dead were counted, with estimates running to 500. Total damage was set at $350 million to $1 billion.

Added to its humane concern was Atlantic management's fear that the fire would reach the waterfront and destroy insured vessels docked there. This anxiety was relieved when the running story of the earthquake and fire appeared in the *New York Sun* while the catastrophe was at its height. The fire had been contained before it could ravage the harbor, the *Sun* reported.

It was generally conceded that the New York paper's account, written at an office less than a mile from Atlantic's New York headquarters by Will Irwin, a native of San Francisco, was the best graphic story of the West Coast tragedy. Working in the *Sun*'s Park Row newsroom and basing his description on bulletins from California editors outside San Francisco and on firsthand knowledge of his native city, as well as facts from government sources, Irwin continued to "cover" the debacle for eight days. His writing exploit came to be known under the title of "The City That Was." It was later published in book form and remained in print more than twenty-five years as a classic of newspaper writing. Atlantic officials appreciated Irwin's coverage, apart from its literary merit, because of early reassurance that marine risks were not affected.

While some twenty insurers went under, this was a vast improvement over the total of seventy companies that failed after the Chicago fire in 1871. Insured losses paid in San Francisco have been estimated at a minimum of $225 million and a maximum of $300 million. Either figure represents an outlay that remained a record until Hurricane Betsy swept across Florida, Louisiana and Mississippi in 1965. By that time, Atlantic was writing all types of coverage and contributed a substantial sum to the new high-loss figure of $715 million incurred by hundreds of insurers.

In Raven's early years as president, one of the most formidable problems facing marine insurers was the underwriting of cotton business. In the crop season of 1899 to 1900, the United States produced 9,535,000 bales and exported 6,090,000 with a monetary value of $241 million.

Although cotton premiums amounted to $10 million or more each year, underwriters steadily lost money on the business. Heavy losses were sustained during the baling process, while the cotton was in storage and during shipping to seaports—not to mention the toll that was taken of the treasure in cargo sent overseas.

To complicate matters, underwriters vied to avoid unattractive business while holding out tempting rate reductions for the preferred risks. The more responsible insurers tried to bring stability and profit into the picture by campaigns for safer methods of handling and shipping and by efforts to halt the rate war. But their exhortations were in vain.

As is often the case, a calamity brought all concerned to their senses and solved the problem. On December 22, 1908, the British steamer *Irada* left Galveston with the most valuable cotton cargo ever shipped from the United States up to that time. But the consignees at Liverpool never set eyes on the record shipment: The *Irada* foundered off the Irish coast. The cargo loss to American and British underwriters was $1,250,000. Atlantic's share was close to $217,000.

This major jolt led to the organization in September, 1909, of the Cotton Reinsurance Exchange—the first marine insurance syndicate. Atlantic, Insurance Company of North America, and United States Lloyd's were the three American members. They were joined by six English companies, and the syndicate, in effect, assumed control of cotton underwriting. It perfected methods of reducing hazard in every phase of the cotton business. Exhaustive surveys were conducted of compresses and warehouses. Those found wanting were deservedly penalized by higher rate charges. This provided incentive for improvements that were not long in coming.

Other studies were conducted by the exchange—on baling, handling during transit and on the docks and on cotton fires at sea. Recommendations and instructions were issued, and when they were observed, premium charges declined. More important, the loss experience improved, and the underwriters as well as the owners profited. The exchange created the Cotton Engineering & Inspection Service in 1916 to continue and to extend the work of technical improvement.

The late Hendon Chubb, head of Chubb & Son Inc. and a legendary name in insurance for more than a half century, said that the organization of the exchange was one of the most constructive accomplishments in the history of the business. Since Mr. Chubb was not given to overstatement, his assessment is significant.

Compliments on the formation of the syndicate came also from an unexpected source. The Government is not noted for the frequency with which it congratulates the insurance fraternity, but the Department of Agriculture was quick to acknowledge the benefits of the exchange and to express its approbation.

In common with other members, Atlantic was gratified by this recognition and took particular satisfaction in its role as a founder of an organization that not only benefited the company itself but also worked to the advantage of the entire insurance business and the country's overall economy.

Raven's tenure had been marked by a number of exciting events involving Atlantic. One of the most notable came in April, 1912, when the proud and "unsinkable" *Titanic* of the White Star Line sailed from Southampton for New York on her maiden voyage.

This new queen of the seas was aptly named; she was titanic in every way: more than 882 feet long, 92 feet wide and 175 feet from her keel to the top of her four huge funnels. This meant that she was as tall as an eleven-story building and four city blocks long. But perhaps her most arresting feature was the novel construction that prompted one of her deckhands to boast that "God himself couldn't sink this ship." His blasphemous optimism was pardonable because the *Titanic* had a double bottom, and she was divided into sixteen compartments formed by watertight bulkheads running clear across the ship. No one could anticipate anything worse than a collision at the juncture of two compartments, and since the *Titanic* could float even if two were flooded, she was labeled "unsinkable." But something worse did happen.

When she steamed out of Southampton on April 10, 1912, with a passenger list of the world's elite, the *Titanic* narrowly missed ramming the American liner *New York* at dockside. This harbinger of disaster was soon forgotten in the festive atmosphere of the maiden voyage.

All went well until April 14 when six separate warnings of ice in the Atlantic reached the *Titanic* from other ships. The last foreboding message came at 11 P.M. from the *California,* but she cut off her wireless before giving the exact location of the ice. The *Titanic* plowed ahead to disaster.

Only 40 minutes later two lookouts saw a large ice mass directly ahead. One rang the crow's-nest bell three times in warning of danger, then phoned the bridge. He reported an iceberg in the ship's path. The two lookouts then stood helplessly at their posts for the next half minute as the *Titanic* neared the wet, glistening berg without turning. Suddenly, the ship's bow swung to port, and the ice appeared to glide swiftly by the starboard side. The lookouts breathed easier; it had been a near miss.

But others aboard knew better. One woman passenger, jolted out of a sound sleep, said it seemed "as though somebody had drawn a giant finger along the side of the ship." The quartermaster, standing watch on the afterdeck, noticed something even more significant: A break in the steady rhythm of the engines. He looked forward and saw what he thought was an ancient windjammer in full sail sweeping along the *Titanic*'s starboard side. A closer look told him it was an iceberg rising 100 feet above the sea. In a moment it had disappeared astern, its grim work done.

In the next frantic hours, the ocean was brightened by a shower of blue-white stars drifting down from distress rockets the *Titanic* fired into the night. Her wireless operator tapped out incessant calls for help. Response was prompt from a number of vessels, but still no help appeared.

Receiving the *Titanic*'s calls was a young wireless operator on the roof of Wanamaker's department store in New York—David Sarnoff, who was destined to become the head of Radio Corporation of America.

In his biography of Sarnoff, published in 1965 by Harper & Row, Eugene Lyons reports that the young man was listening casually to a routine flood of dots and dashes. Suddenly he was stung to startled attention. The message was dim and faraway and choked by static, but he deciphered it, notwithstanding. It was coming from the S.S. *Olympic*, 1,400 miles away:

"S.S. *Titanic* ran into iceberg. Sinking fast."

Sarnoff signaled receipt of the message and asked the *Olympic* for details. He notified the press. Soon "extras" were being cried in the streets, and the eyes of the whole world, it seemed, along with its fears and hopes, were fixed on Sarnoff and his earphones. Reporters, then crowds of friends and relatives of those on board the liner, along with the curious, converged on the department store. Police had to be summoned to control them and to give the operator the privacy and quiet that he needed.

Other coastal stations and vessels in the disaster area tried to help, which merely jammed the airwaves. This was to be a one-man job. President William Howard Taft ordered all other stations to close down so that the one at Wanamaker's might more easily maintain communications.

For three days and three nights, without sleep and virtually without food, Sarnoff remained glued to the earphones while a horrified world hung on his every word.

The reports from the *Olympic* were primarily the names of survivors as they were hauled from the ocean by radio-equipped ships that had rushed to the scene. Not until he had given the press the names of the last survivors, 72 hours after he had picked up the first distress signal, did the exhausted operator relinquish his post.

The stark drama of the scene—a young man in Manhattan as the sole contact with a great catastrophe in midocean—made a terrific impression on the public mind. Radio, which had been a scientific curiosity, was raised in a few days to the status of a necessity. Hundreds more could have been saved if ships in the area, several of them closer to the *Titanic* than those that did hurry to the rescue, had been equipped to hear the distress call. This sad fact was too obvious and too devastating not to register.

Life had been saved at sea by wireless in the past, without erasing public apathy on the subject. But after the *Titanic* tragedy Congress quickly passed a radio act that made it mandatory for ships carrying more than fifty persons to install radio and to maintain a constant watch at sea. It also prescribed the licensing of operators and regular inspection of the equipment.

At 2:20 A.M. on April 15, the *Titanic* sank.

Another hour went by before those drifting in the lifeboats were cheered by a burst of rockets from the Cunard liner *Carpathia*. Working through the night, her crew picked up more than 700 survivors and headed for New York at 8:50 A.M. The British Board of Trade set the loss of life at 1,503, the most reliable figure. Later, the world learned that the *Titanic*'s lifeboats would hold only 1,178 of the 2,207 on board.

Of the $140,000 in insurance placed in the American market on the hull of the *Titanic*, Atlantic carried $100,000. This claim was paid within a week. After the *Titanic*'s tragic end, the advertising of luxury liners for long years made no reference to the word "unsinkable." But by 1956, that was the very term applied, even by experts, to the *Andrea Doria*, the pride of Italy's reviving merchant marine.

She was equipped with the most modern electronic devices to prevent accidents at sea. But as she headed for New York, she collided with the Swedish-American liner *Stockholm* off Nantucket Island and sank on the morning of July 26, 1956, with the loss of fifty-one lives. Atlantic had a generous share of the loss—$150,000.

Atlantic underwriters, of course, took both financial losses in stride. Unlike a gullible public, they knew that neither of these vessels nor any other that ever came down the ways was unsinkable. If a craft with that quality ever appeared, there would be no need for marine insurers. No Atlantic man would ever subscribe to the view of the *Titanic* deckhand who boasted that even the Almighty could not send his ship to the bottom. They rather agree with the prayer of the humble Breton fisherman:

> *O Lord, have mercy on us,*
> *For Thy sea is so vast*
> *And my boat is so small.*

The *Titanic* tragedy, although one of the great sagas of the sea, proved to be only an anticlimactic event of the presidency of Anton A. Raven. He was still directing the company's operations when the world was engulfed in war in the summer of 1914. Atlantic faced the problems of the conflict under the leadership of a man in his eighty-first year.

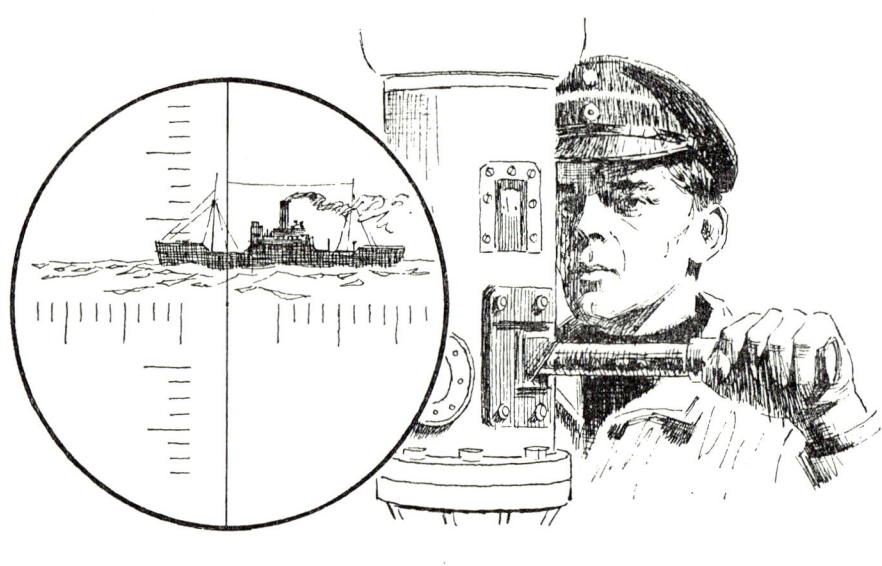

Crises: World War and Depression

On July 31, 1914, the New York Stock Exchange—the unfailing barometer of world events—confirmed that war was imminent by suspending operations to avert a panic. Within the week, Germany had declared war on Russia and France. England then came into the conflict against Germany, as did Japan.

American marine insurers were thrust into a new and frightening situation. Never in history had there been a war involving such tremendous sea power on both sides. American experience with war risk had been limited to the Spanish-American, the Russo-Japanese and the Civil wars. The marine problems of these conflicts paled by comparison with the threat now posed by giant nations on the seas.

Frantic demands for war coverage poured into New York, and the capacity of the marine market was soon overtaxed. Rates rocketed. It must be remembered that the United States was not then a belligerent.

The immediate problem was to cover risks already at sea in the early days of the war—many of them under the German flag. They were hurrying for haven in neutral ports around the world.

Wireless was well established by this time, so the vessels of belligerent nations knew of their danger at once, and the protection was quickly sought.

The insurers began writing war-risk insurance in 1914 under the same terms they had granted in former wars. The coverage was complete against capture, seizure and destruction by men-of-war of all belligerent nations. It soon became apparent, however, that British naval power was overwhelming. German shipping was relentlessly hounded, and neutral ships had small chance of reaching German ports.

This resulted in the world marine market's adoption of what was known as the Free of British Capture clause in the policies. Many severe losses were sustained before this proviso became effective.

Atlantic had trouble even after its adoption. President Raven disdained the use of any policy provision that indicated fear of the English. He accepted substantial lines on cargoes destined for countries adjacent to Germany, and he deliberately omitted the Free of British Capture precaution.

He soon had Atlantic committed for perilous amounts, and his alarmed but helpless colleagues feared that the company would be ruined. A member of the staff telephoned James Brown, a trustee, and acquainted him with the situation. Mr. Brown hurried to the office for a conference with the president, but no results of his visit were apparent.

It remained for the redoubtable Charles E. Fay and a willing confederate, young Winter, to solve the problem. They stayed at the office long hours in the evening, stamping the Free of British Capture clause on the risks Raven had accepted during the day. Later, they notified the policyholder or the broker of this additional condition. By this action, Fay and Winter ran the risk of losing their positions. However, they must have reasoned that if the president were allowed to continue his reckless underwriting, Atlantic would go under and there would be no jobs in any case.

The problem was permanently solved when Raven was induced to relinquish the presidency early in 1915 to take the then honorary post of chairman. He was succeeded by Cornelius Eldert who was nearing his sixty-sixth birthday when he took office. He was a Long Islander and had been with the company since he was sixteen years of age. His forte was loss adjusting, but he had a broad knowledge of the marine business, keen judgment and great powers of concentration. The only element lacking in his leadership when he became president was the spirit of innovation, which is understandable in view of his age and background.

Eldert had a baptism of fire as the new chief executive. He not only had to cope with a world war but he faced a private one conducted by his predecessor. The former president clung to his old desk and insisted on coming to the office every day to spend most of his time glowering at his successor.

One day, word was received from his home that he was confined with a cold. The next morning was raw and rainy, and the office force was astonished to see Raven appear at his usual time. As he passed Eldert's desk, he was greeted politely by the new president: "Why, Mr. Raven, we didn't expect you down this morning." Raven replied with a growl and seated himself. After glaring at Eldert several moments, he jumped from his chair, rushed over, shook his fist in his successor's face and shouted: "I'll have you know that I have just as much right to be here as you have!"

Eldert showed remarkable tolerance in dealing with the situation as it became more and more aggravating. Finally, his patience and temper exhausted, he told Raven that if he did not cease his annoying behavior, he would tender his resignation to the trustees and give them his reasons. Raven's belligerency subsided from that day on, but he never forgave Eldert for being president.

The doughty little Dutchman lived until 1919. Despite his peculiarities he had served the company well. Under his administration Atlantic had an almost unbroken succession of prosperous years. Shortly after his death, the *Weekly Underwriter* said of him: "His convictions were strong and he was not easily influenced. He made up his mind quickly and once he had done so, he was adamant in his adherence to his conclusions. Of exceptional authority and decision, he had a strong influence upon those with whom he came in contact, and his place in the administration of this company was commanding and peculiarly his own." Anyone who had ever worked with Raven could say Amen to this statement, particularly to the concluding words.

Eldert was also a man with strong characteristics—frugality being the chief of them. The high windows in Atlantic's first-floor executive offices and the poor heating made the desks near the windows a cold place to work. Storm sashes had been made for these windows, but Eldert would not permit them to be used. He feared the other tenants in the building would demand similar protection. Conditions in the summer were equally trying. On one occasion, an application for insurance had blown through an open window during the summer and was returned by a passerby. Eldert promptly ordered that all windows be kept closed. Atlantic's management and staff sweltered for years under these conditions before the order was at long last countermanded.

When war was declared on Germany by the United States in April, 1917, practically every office building in lower New York except Atlantic's displayed the American flag. Eldert was fearful of inciting trouble with elements of the large German population in the city, and he ruled that the emblem was not to be flown. In some way, Edmund Bayliss, a trustee, learned of the situation, called on the president and told him the banner should be displayed. Eldert acceded but, according to the ever-watchful Bogardus, a witness to the incident, he was hopping mad at being overruled.

Eldert's conservatism—illustrated by these minor incidents—was undoubtedly a major factor in his able leadership of the company throughout the war. In 1915 the United States had established a Government war-risk office to provide coverage at subsidized rates. This bureau was set up by men from the marine insurance business and was a unit of the U. S. Treasury Department. It served a useful purpose during the hostilities, but at no time did it eliminate the need for private coverage, the demand for which remained strong at all times.

Atlantic took a leading role in meeting the demand. This was not a simple task, for chaotic conditions prevailed during the war. There were no satisfactory reinsurance facilities. The British marine market was hard pressed, and there were no arrangements by which business could be pooled to spread the risk and afford a broader market. Companies had to go it largely on their own. This was reflected in Atlantic's volume, which swelled in 1917 to $11 million—owing mainly to large war-risk premiums.

Before American entry into the conflict, from 1914 through 1916, this country's exports of explosives were up from $6 million to $467 million. Exports of iron and steel were doubled, and other commodities showed greater rises. Thus the underwriters' problems were complicated. In spite of uncharted and unfamiliar areas, with vast values at stake and with fearsome perils such as submarines to be considered, Eldert and his officers adopted plans liberal enough to protect the interest of policyholders against the unparalleled emergencies and conservative enough to maintain unimpaired Atlantic's financial strength.

The record speaks for itself: In 1914 the company insured a total sum in marine and war risks of close to $738 million. By 1916 this rose to $1.09 billion. The figure remained over a billion in 1917 and sank to $779 million in 1918. Dividends through 1914 to 1918 were 40%.

The demand for war risk was so great that many large fire companies established marine departments, thus expanding available markets. Most of the companies that entered the business during the war remained in it.

This helped to alleviate the demand for marine coverages after the war, but even more capacity was needed. American shipping had faded in the years before the conflict so that when hostilities began, the country was carrying only about 10% of its commerce in its own bottoms. But during the war the merchant marine expanded rapidly with all types of vessels, including a "bridge of wooden ships" created to span the Atlantic. The emergency-built tonnage called for a strong active marine market in the United States.

In 1920, leading underwriters, Eldert and his vice-president, Walter W. Parsons, among them, were called to Washington by the Merchant Marine and Fisheries Committee of Congress. This unit suggested the formation of a syndicate whereby hull coverage could be handled through one source. Enabling legislation was passed, and the American Hull Insurance Syndicate was born. Government interest was in the vessels only and not in cargo. The syndicate was available to all ocean-going ships flying the American flag. In later years, especially during World War II, its scope was enlarged to include foreign hulls. The organization started with forty-seven companies subscribing for various percentages of business on the basis of their financial standing and their individual desire to participate. Atlantic was required to take its share of syndicated business on a nondividend basis. Today, the organization is one of the principal hull markets of the world, and there are more than seventy member companies.

After the war, Eldert's life was brightened when American insurers received substantial reparations from the German government in reimbursement for losses, the underwriters having succeeded to the recovery rights of the insured following payment of the war claims. Atlantic's share of the awards amounted to $3,300,000, including interest to January 1, 1928. Accrued interest since that date to June, 1957, amounted to $1,397,000. Atlantic paid counsel fees and other legal expenses incurred in the recovery of about $300,000. The company had collected, net of expenses, to June of 1957, $2,540,000, while $1,800,000 including interest, remained to be paid as of that date. Atlantic thus fared much better in World War I than in the case of the *Alabama* Claims.

Despite his fears about flying the American flag at the beginning of the war, no one ever doubted Eldert's personal courage. He demonstrated it on September 16, 1920.

Eldert was sitting on his raised platform directly under two large windows at the center of the Wall Street end of the building. He was signing loss warrants when the bells of Trinity Church tolled noon. The president put down his pen, leaned back in his chair and took his watch from his vest pocket to check its accuracy. At that moment, a terrific blast rocked Wall Street. The windows on that side of the office were blown out; those on the William Street side were sucked in.

After the blast, Eldert stood a few feet away from his desk, methodically brushing glass from his hair. A long jagged spear of glass quivered upright on his desk top. It had pierced his signature on the last loss warrant he had signed. Standing upright in the leather seat of Vice-President Fay's chair was a huge triangular arrow of glass. Fortunately the busy Fay had been in another part of the room. No one in Atlantic's office was injured.

The employees rushed out—it was lunch hour, but they could not have been restrained in any case—to discover a scene of carnage a few doors westward on Wall Street. Someone whose identity and motives are unknown to this day had left a horse-drawn wagon with a bomb set to go off at noon when Wall Street crowds would be at their height. If the timing had been 5 minutes later, the calamity would have been far greater since many Wall Street employees had not reached the street by noon. As it was, 30 were killed, 100 injured and a toll of $2 million in property damage was taken.

After the war there was a boom in ocean shipping because American goods, which had been off the market while the war lasted, were again available to meet the demands of many markets, particularly South America. This meant an increasing volume of marine premiums. Companies were writing the business freely on broad terms. However, following a tremendous expansion of exports through 1921, there was a crash in the commodity market due to overproduction and excess purchases. There was a resulting drastic drop in prices, and many foreign buyers repudiated their contracts. Goods on dock and on shore in foreign countries, notably South America and Cuba, were allowed to remain in the open as the buyers failed to live up to commitments. Losses from theft, pilferage and weather damage were extremely heavy, causing many of the companies new to the business and without a solid marine background to abandon the market.

Atlantic—with all its experience—had some heavy losses. One was the Consolidated Steel account. Big shipments had gone to Buenos Aires and Brazil. When the smash came and contracts were repudiated, large quantities of corrugated steel sheets, intended for building purposes, were left in the open at destination and became so badly rusted that they were unfit for use. These sheets had been considered covered during delay and were insured against fresh water since by that time the company was beginning to broaden its contracts to cover hazards other than those stipulated in the basic originally restricted policies.

Theft and pilferage became such threats that on shipments of revolvers to South America the company was receiving as much as 25% and 30% on the risks and still losing money.

All sorts of ships were being pressed into service, many of them operating on a shoestring. One was the steamer *Poznan*. It had a large assorted cargo for Cuba. The ship could not discharge this immediately since the owners were without funds to pay the crew. They brought the ship back to Baltimore and left her unattended. Large quantities of goods were stolen, including a consignment of Gillette blades insured by Atlantic.

But probably the heaviest losses ever suffered by the company on one account within a short period were the total losses on Cuban shipments of the National Sugar Refining Co. The steamer *Santiago*, carrying cargo worth more than $600,000, was lost in the spring of 1924, and the *Glendon* went down several months later with sugar valued at $438,000. Both claims were promptly paid.

Even more drastic losses — unconnected with underwriting — lay ahead for the company. In the mid-1920s, while Europe was struggling with economic reverses, the United States was enjoying its biggest boom. The public, confident that there would be no end to the new age of prosperity, seemed to believe that all basic economic laws had been repealed. Overoptimistic business leaders and economic seers contributed to this delusion.

The public was even more misled by a rising stock market that seemed to have no ceiling. Those who could borrow—and the number included nearly everyone in that freewheeling day—rushed to acquire shares. Thus, while the stock index climbed higher and higher, the amount of brokers' loans ominously ascended with it. By the summer of 1929, hundreds of millions of shares were carried on margin. Some conservative publications and financial organizations began to sound warnings of trouble ahead, but they were laughed at for their pains. Everyone was an expert on the market, and many were wealthy—at least on paper.

The mass dream of unending plenty ended in a nightmare in October, 1929. On the 24th day of that month, close to 13 million shares were traded with heavy losses in the wildest day ever seen on the New York Stock Exchange. Still, the optimists were not convinced until five days later when the market completely collapsed under the weight of a 16 million share day. Personal savings and resources of many businesses were wiped out. The greatest depression in United States history followed.

The grim story is graphically told in the fluctuation of the stocks of the country's leading enterprises in a period of little more than two months:

	High Price, September 3, 1929	Low Price, November 13, 1929
American Can	181⅞	86
A.T.&T.	304	197¼
Anaconda Copper	131½	70
Electric Bond & Share	186¾	50¼
General Electric	396¼	168⅛
General Motors	72¾	36
Montgomery Ward	137⅞	49¼
New York Central	256⅜	160
Radio Corp.	101	28
Union Carbide & Carbon	137⅞	59
U. S. Steel	261¾	150
Westinghouse	289⅞	102⅝
Woolworth	100⅜	52¼

A broader picture of the debacle is provided by the plunge of the Dow-Jones industrial average from 381 in September of 1929 to 198 in November and to a bottom of 41 in July of 1932. In the same intervals, the rail average plummeted from 189 to 128 and then to a low of 13.

At that time, Atlantic was a large holder of railroad stocks and bonds and of bank issues. All were considered prime investments, but they did not escape the fate of other securities in the market break.

At the end of 1928, Atlantic's investments had a book value of about $7 million. The market value was approximately $15.8 million. As 1931 ended, the company had bought additional securities to bring the book value up to $9.1 million. But the market value by then had fallen to $10,175,000.

Many insurers were so weakened by the crash that producers who had business to place carried at all times a list of companies that their organizations approved. While Atlantic always appeared on such lists, the stock market break fortified the management in its belief that an insurance company cannot depend solely on the investment market for growth and progress.

Miles F. York, the tenth president, has reiterated this truth frequently in recent times; in 1962 he made it one of the primary operating principles of the company when he amended the guidelines under

The *Titanic*, called the "Millionaires' Special" by the press, was four city blocks long and eleven stories high. Protected by the most ingenious safety devices, she was regarded as "unsinkable." On April 10, 1912, she slipped out of Southampton on her maiden voyage to New York. Less than five days later she went down in 12,000 feet of icy water, 300 feet of her hull ripped open by a massive iceberg. Of the $140,000 placed in the American insurance market on the majestic liner's hull, Atlantic Mutual carried $100,000.

which Atlantic operates, with this statement: "The Atlantic Companies will continue to be underwriting companies. Underwriting is not to be sacrificed for volume."

This firm declaration takes on added significance when it is recalled that it was made at the very time when the insurance industry had relaxed many of its standards in the quest for premiums to be invested in a booming market, with the hope of offsetting underwriting losses.

Cornelius Eldert died in 1930 after giving his best to the company since 1865. He was replaced by Walter W. Parsons, who had served an "interesting" apprenticeship as Raven's assistant. As important as the accession of the new president were the promotion of Winter to first vice-president and the simultaneous naming of Bogardus as second vice-president. The two latter moves insured Atlantic's revival and the renewal of its original spirit.

The Winter-Bogardus Years

President Parsons took charge of a company that had been standing stock-still in nearly all important respects for more than a quarter century. In the early 1900s, Atlantic was the leading marine insurer in the United States and one of the largest in the world. In 1904 premiums totaled $2.09 million. In 1930 on Eldert's death, they were $3.1 million.

Of course the volume had boomed during World War I when war-risk coverage sent the figures higher. But the totals for the more comparable years of 1904 and 1930 illustrated Atlantic's lack of growth.

Parsons was fifty-six when he took office. A native of Hoosick Falls, New York, he was educated at Trinity College in Hartford. He then became associated with Mather & Co., a Philadelphia agency that represented Atlantic, and remained there ten years before Raven invited him to join the company as his assistant. Parsons' mild and unaggressive personality must have been one of the reasons Raven selected him. The Dutchman disliked those with strong traits matching his own. Winter was the prime example. But Parsons was an ideal associate.

His presidency began with a rather frightening experience. For some years there had been heavy trading in the company's scrip. Insured merchants and shipowners often needed cash for their business operations, and they found an eager market for their scrip dividends. Brisk trading in the valuable certificates ensued.

This meant potential trouble because the voting power for the election of trustees was not lodged with the policyholders but in the certificates themselves. The "outside" scripholders posed a threat; they could name the management and gain control of the company. This ominous possibility came to a head shortly after Parsons took office.

Banking institutions, acting as trustees, often held fairly large amounts of scrip. While it was redeemable at any time by order of the Atlantic trustees and was subject only to such interest as might be declared annually, in practice the scrip had always run for several years and the rate of interest had been 6% over the years. Thus it was regarded as a prime short-term investment.

The Irving Trust Co. in New York held about a million dollars of the scrip, and proxies had been sent to the bank for signature for the election of Atlantic trustees to be held at the annual meeting. As time went by and the proxies were not returned, Atlantic's officers became somewhat disturbed, fearing that possibly the trust company was withholding the proxies in an attempt to elect its own slate of trustees and eventually gain control of the company.

Finally, Parsons went to see the president of the Irving Trust to determine why the proxies had not been executed. The president of Irving Trust said that he had simply overlooked the matter and that he would be happy to sign the proxies and send them in, which he did.

Parsons and his colleagues were relieved. The experience, however, strengthened their opinion that it was unwise to leave the voting power in the scrip itself. Although it would have taken at least three annual elections for outsiders to gain control of the company and the trustees could have made it difficult by calling for redemption of outstanding scrip, such a contest would have been completely out of character with Atlantic practices. The problem was later resolved in the amended charter, which provided that policyholders should elect the trustees.

Parsons soon proved that he was an astute judge of Atlantic's needs for long-term development. Although Raven had predicted that if Winter were ever given high rank in management he would wreck the organization, Parsons gave full rein to his vice-president. He foresaw that this forceful man would restore the company's fortunes. Winter, in effect, became the leader of the plans and changes that marked Parsons' short term. Working as a team, they proceeded to maneuver Atlantic into a better competitive stance. They were well prepared for the task. For years they had discussed the future of the company and formulated plans for giving it a new lease on life.

By coincidence, Atlantic's charter required renewal shortly after Parsons took office. He and Winter reviewed this document and had it rewritten with one basic purpose in mind: Gradual expansion of the company's operations.

Winter had long chafed under the competitive disadvantage of the scrip-participating policies the company had issued since inception. They carried a higher premium charge than the rates in the general marine market. The first order of business was to eliminate this handicap. This was done by a proviso in the new charter permitting issuance of policies on a cash-participating basis so that Atlantic's rates would be in line with those of stock-company competitors.

The policyholders were given a choice of continuing on the old scrip plan or of accepting the new cash-participating method. A considerable majority immediately selected the cash option, and, as time went by, more and more policyholders expressed the same preference.

With the scrip drying up, some of the trustees asked Parsons and Winter why they did not call in all the certificates and save the 6% interest. The two men considered this unfair. They pointed out that traditionally the holders anticipated retaining the scrip with its generous interest for five years. There was no obligation on Atlantic's part to go along with this custom, but, in keeping with its principles, that is exactly what was done. The last of the scrip was not called in and paid off until 1940.

Winter had long since resolved that if Atlantic was to move ahead in a modern insurance world, it would be necessary to add other forms of coverage to its marine lines. Fire insurance powers were therefore reinstated in the amended charter. This was a harbinger of Winter's long and determined fight to give insurers the right to sell multiple lines of protection.

Atlantic did not plunge into the fire business or other unfamiliar areas at once. The approach adopted was to move into new fields related to ocean marine. Yacht coverage was the first new venture. While this was not a daring departure, it did bring Atlantic into the area of personal insurance. All of its prior experience had been with commercial policyholders. With the addition of the yacht line, the company began dealing with an entirely new "public." The experience gained in transactions with this personal market proved valuable not too many years later when a large share of Atlantic's volume was represented by policies on homes, automobiles and other individual possessions.

Next came a much more important step that not only took the company into a flourishing phase of insurance but led to future eminence in the field of inland marine. This rather undescriptive term has been unscientifically defined as the insurance of anything that moves on, over or under land. But it is much more than that. It also includes coverage on tunnels and bridges; on jewelry and furs; on paintings, sculpture and other fine arts; on registered mail; on industrial equipment while it is being installed; on air cargo; and on a host of other exposures.

Atlantic had been left at the post in the 1920s when other insurers were exploiting every aspect of inland marine and developing new and broader policies for a booming market. In keeping with its unadventurous attitude, the company had confined its writings to transportation of goods by rail or water. Meanwhile, competitors had lapped up the cream of the business.

This was the sort of situation calculated to rile Winter. He was delighted to be assigned the task of finding a man who could make the company a factor in this profitable area. Winter had scarcely begun looking for his man when an unexpected inquiry came from the Yale University placement bureau, stating that one of the university's graduates—an experienced inland underwriter—was seeking a connection with a mutual insurer.

The young man who came to see Winter in response to an invitation was Franklin B. Tuttle. He had an impressive background. For five years he had been with the American Foreign Insurance Association, first in New York City and then at Trieste, Italy, where he gained an international outlook and a knowledge of several phases of insurance. He had then joined the Insurance Company of North America where he had received his inland marine grounding and experience.

Tuttle, a native of Naugatuck, Connecticut, has always had two outstanding characteristics: Laconic expression with unmistakable meaning and the appraising attitude of the underwriter. The latter quality led him to the decision that in Atlantic he had found the right company. Winter, an equally shrewd judge, decided he had found the right man. Thus began an association that not only brought Atlantic into prominence among inland marine insurers but led to Tuttle's rise to the presidency in 1951 and two years later to chairman and chief executive officer, a post he was to hold for thirteen years.

Parsons and Winter methodically pressed on with their development program. They realized that to succeed in the yacht and inland marine fields, wide sources of business were indispensable. It was obvious that there would have to be a change in the outmoded practice of conducting practically all operations from the home office.

Since 1856 Atlantic had maintained an agency in Boston, but all underwriting decisions were made in New York. In 1931 the Boston facility was converted into a branch office. Other branch and service units were opened in the next few years at Philadelphia, Cleveland, Chicago and Baltimore—prime seaport locations, as well as strategic centers for development of all types of business in the years ahead.

Without doubt, Winter would have pushed ahead even more vigorously. He confirms this in his reminiscences:

"Mr. Parsons told me on more than one occasion when I suggested some further extension of the company's activities according to the pattern we had discussed during the previous regime, that he had become president too late in life. He said he lacked the courage to make the ventures which 10 years before seemed a natural development of the company's activities. Nevertheless, he did not abandon the plans; they were merely postponed to what might appear a more suitable time."

The fact is that Parsons had given Winter his head to a surprising degree. Whether the president would have gone further at a "more suitable time" is a question that will never be answered, for Parsons underwent what was thought to be minor surgery in the fifth year of his term and unexpectedly died in 1934. Less than two weeks later, Winter found himself president of Atlantic, charged with its management at a time when it was in the middle of what he called its "metamorphosis."

The forty-nine-year-old Winter was the first Atlantic president under the age of fifty since John D. Jones took office in 1855. The election of Bogardus as Winter's vice-president was equally fortunate for Atlantic. He was an invaluable counselor to the aggressive president, and although he was also progressive, his stability was an ideal counterbalance to the uncommon force and drive of Winter.

Many years later, when Bogardus marked his 50th anniversary with Atlantic in 1954, Winter summed up the pair's effectiveness as a team with one of his characteristically acute phrases: "Alike enough and yet different enough," was his description. He went on to recall their enduring friendship that flourished more than half a century.

When they took Atlantic's helm, the two had been colleagues for thirty years. They had spent many an hour speculating on the opportunities for broadening operations into the entire field of property-casualty insurance. They were confident of their ability to do so, but they shared one reservation. They wondered if the trustees, accustomed to conservative management, would back their rather advanced ideas.

This doubt was ill-founded. The trustees had kept an eye on Winter for some time, particularly since 1930 when he became a power in the company on Eldert's passing. They liked what they saw, and they were also impressed by the more reticent but obviously able Bogardus. The two got the full backing of the board, and they proceeded to convert their dream into reality.

This was not easily done. The company had long depended on the comparatively few brokers in the ocean marine field for its business. When it began seeking other producers to build yacht and inland marine volume, Atlantic found that they were difficult to attract. The same discouraging response was encountered in 1935 when Atlantic set up a new department to conduct a full-scale fire insurance operation. Years of intensive effort through unrelenting production programs backed by skillful advertising were necessary before premiums from the new lines would begin to mount.

But Winter and Bogardus were not able to devote their full attention to internal affairs. The world was nearing another holocaust. As always, marine underwriters with their international interests were quick to sense the danger. They uneasily watched the rise of Hitler in the early 1930s, and they were not deceived in the fall of 1938 when the false promises made at Munich persuaded many that war could be averted. By the spring of 1939, the marine market was convinced that a general conflict was inevitable.

The marine business took immediate action. The American Cargo War Risk Reinsurance Exchange was organized and in full operation by June, 1939. This organization, in which each subscriber pooled its war-risk cargo business and then took out an agreed percentage to carry for its own account, proved to be a bulwark. Atlantic was the only mutual member, but Winter became chairman of the exchange and head of the executive committee. Bogardus was on the underwriting committee, and Percy Craig, another Atlantic vice-president, was chairman of the exchange's loss committee.

War insurance on hulls was another matter. In the early days of the war, the American Hull Insurance Syndicate assumed this business. But in a single month, all the profits the syndicate had accumulated since its formation in 1920 were wiped out by the frightful toll being taken on the seas. Atlantic's volume of marine business in proportion to its total premiums was larger by far than that of most insurers, and as a substantial member of the syndicate, the company was more severely tested than any other.

Ships were being sunk at an increasing rate—often fifteen to twenty a day. But the syndicate held on until the Government assumed the hull business through a war-risk office a few months after America became a belligerent when the Japanese bombed Pearl Harbor on December 7, 1941.

By this time, however, the cargo losses sustained through the exchange were so tremendous that several of the largest members threatened to withdraw. This would have meant the end of the organization and chaos in the marine market. At a meeting in the early summer of 1942, Winter took the platform and told the fearful exchange members that they could not abdicate the responsibility they had assumed. He assured them that the results could not be as bad as they seemed. His confidence and the support of his friends Hendon Chubb of Chubb & Son and John A. Diemand of Insurance Company of North America sustained the subscribers and saved the shaky arrangement. Moreover, he proved to be an astute judge of the situation, for when accurate figures became available it was learned that the tide had turned a month before he delivered the speech that preserved the exchange. No accomplishment of Winter's long and notable career exceeded this typical example of outstanding leadership in time of crisis.

In April, 1942, Atlantic marked its 100th anniversary. No less appropriate time could have been found for this event. Submarine marauders on all the oceans of the world were terrorizing shipping. Atlantic's management was spending sleepless nights and was in anything but the festive mood associated with a centenary.

Nevertheless, the management proceeded with plans long in the making. One was the organization of a stock affiliate to accept part of the profitable reinsurance Atlantic had been placing with other companies. Thus, in the latter part of 1941, arrangements were made to incorporate such a company, and in the anniversary year the Centennial Insurance Company—named in honor of the parent company's birthday—began operations.

The wholly-owned subsidiary was not only successful from the start but developments in the insurance business in the next two years led Atlantic to extend the scope of Centennial. It was expanded into a primary insurer to accept business on its own account. Significantly, this was written through a sales force of independent agents.

Organization on the agency basis was made feasible by the decision of the U. S. Supreme Court in the Southeastern Underwriters Association case that insurance was interstate commerce and subject to antitrust laws. The ensuing relaxation of traditional rules that restricted agency appointments provided an ideal climate for the Atlantic organization to make rapid strides in building the strong agency force that is now a main source of its business.

Winter and Bogardus had long entertained the idea of entering the casualty field. But under the laws of that day, neither Atlantic nor Centennial could write that class. Winter had been hopeful that the laws would be changed to permit a single company to write multiple lines of coverage and that Atlantic could defer its participation in the casualty business until that time. But legislators were slow to act. Meanwhile, the casualty companies in their quest for expanded volume were vigorously seeking inland marine business, which they were permitted to write. Atlantic was unable to protect its interests, and it became apparent that for defensive purposes, if no other, it was imperative to organize a casualty unit.

Accordingly, in 1944, Atlantic Mutual Indemnity Company was formed. When it began operations in 1945, the Atlantic group was able for the first time in its long history to write all forms of property and liability insurance.

Meanwhile, Winter and Bogardus had been extending operations into additional states. There was constant pressure from producers on the Pacific Coast to make Atlantic facilities available. But the company was not interested in doing business there until it could set up its own fully staffed office.

This seemed a rather forlorn hope. There was a dearth of competent men trained on the West Coast and familiar with conditions there. Nevertheless, Winter and Bogardus located a prospect within a year and in the most unexpected place, New York City. In discovering him, they also found a future Atlantic president.

The man was Miles F. York, a Californian with twenty-three years experience with the Fireman's Fund Insurance Company as an ocean and inland marine underwriter. He had been at the Fund home office in San Francisco twenty years before his transfer in 1942 to New York, where he caught the eye of Atlantic's management.

York is a large man whose characteristic facial expression is one of amiable skepticism. His outstanding trait is complete candor. This is never intended unkindly, but anyone not looking for a forthright answer would be well advised not to ask for his opinion. In short, he looks like an underwriter, and acts and speaks like one. These qualities—and the record of accomplishment that went with them—prompted Winter and Bogardus late in 1944 to invite York to join the company.

In January, 1945, he became vice-president and general manager of the Pacific division, which he was charged with organizing. By May, he had opened the first office in San Francisco. In the next four-and-a-half years, other units were operating in Los Angeles, Seattle and Portland. Two years later, York was back at Atlantic's home office as executive vice-president and a director, and in 1953 he became the tenth president.

In 1946, Winter had concluded that the company's era of basic expansion was coming to a close. It was active in all property-liability lines, and its facilities had been extended from coast to coast.

Characteristically, Winter decided it was time for him to transfer his still considerable energies to the growing problems of general management that expansion presented. To do so, he would have to be relieved of the responsibility of conducting Atlantic's day-to-day affairs.

The trustees recreated the post of chairman, once held by Raven, but this time on a meaningful basis, and in the charter carefully designated the occupant as the senior officer of the corporation. Winter, then only sixty-one, moved up to the new post. Bogardus became president at fifty-nine, and Tuttle advanced in the line of succession as executive vice-president at forty-five. Associated with them was a group of young men with a voice in the active management of the company.

By these management maneuvers, Winter proved that his often-expressed antipathy to perpetuation in office was not mere talk. He had realized his great ambition of seeing the Atlantic enterprise conducted by younger men and had opened the paths of progress for those lower in rank in the company.

The Winter-Bogardus years—and this is an accurate term, for the two cannot be disassociated in the leadership of Atlantic's era of recovery—ended with the close of 1952 when the management of the company was turned over to Tuttle as chairman and York as president. No superlatives are needed to emphasize the progress that had been made. In 1952, premium volume was up to $24 million. Assets were $55 million, and surplus was $18 million. There were 24 branches and 908 employees. Atlantic was back on course.

While Winter had been critical of past management that had been unwilling to embark on new enterprises, he was well aware of the contributions his more conservative predecessors had made. He paid them a deserved tribute in his modest commentary on the accomplishments of his regime:

"All of this development is little more than the building of a more modern edifice on the foundation securely laid by those able men who, down through the century past, made the Atlantic name stand for that which was finest in the conduct of a business enterprise."

Winter thus expressed the philosophy that still motivates the management: Progress is impossible without underlying quality, and it is not worth achieving at the price of abandoning principles.

Modernizing the Business

Winter was a man born to break barriers. Trained in ocean marine insurance, which operates on the principle of providing "all risks" protection, he became an early critic of state laws that forced fire companies to restrict their business to certain coverages and kept the casualty insurers in a somewhat similar strait jacket.

The result was a "compartmented" business. Limited by law as to the variety of products they could offer, the two types of insurers had little incentive for innovation, even in their respective specialties. They grew as separate enterprises.

The absurdity of the situation was emphasized by the formation of insurance groups. A fire company would set up a casualty running mate—or vice versa—and the overall organization was able to expand its volume.

However, these groups were merely a combination of completely separate internal companies. The officials of each were often jealous of their prerogatives in the corporate family. They seldom if ever cooperated in bringing better service to the public. This was a highly uneconomic method for one organization to furnish what was in essence a common product. More important, buyers in a growing economy were denied the benefits that would have been possible through a unified insurer.

The main reason for this strangulating method of conducting business was the Appleton rule in New York State. This not only forbade a company of one type from engaging in the business of the other in New York but forced any insurer that wished to do business there to accept the same stricture in every other state. Since companies of consequence had to do business in the vast New York market, the pattern was set for the entire country. This meant that at the very time when all the other industries in the United States were expanding as never before, with greater and more complex coverage needs, the insurance business was lagging far behind in providing them most efficiently.

The inland marine underwriters—free of the shackles that held their fire and casualty counterparts—had shown initiative in expanding their contracts to provide broader protection. This was natural since that business was an outgrowth of ocean marine. But when the "unorthodox" inland operators began treading on the toes of the fire and casualty companies, it was decided that the mavericks must be controlled. The result was a nationwide definition of the power and scope of the inland marine underwriters. This accomplished its primary purpose: Inland marine insurance was well boxed in. All sectors of the business were thrust back into their compartments, and the antiquated mono-line system of operation was reinforced.

In 1942, the National Association of Insurance Commissioners, responding to increasing agitation for broad multiple line powers for fire, casualty and marine companies, named a committee of eight, representing a cross section of the business, to work on the problem. Winter was a member.

This unit came in with its first report within a year. It recommended gradual granting of multiple line powers, and these became effective in many states between 1944 and 1947. The trend was set. The turning point came when New York adopted a full multiple line law in 1949.

The role Winter played in these efforts may be measured by a homely incident. At a dinner in the University Club in New York, attended by the then Insurance Superintendent Robert E. Dineen of New York and members of his department, the pen used by Governor Dewey in signing the new law was officially presented to Winter.

As one of the crusaders for multiple line powers, he was determined that the insurance business would keep step with the rest of American industry in developing new products, putting them on the market and constantly improving them.

He had been vexed for years by the lethargy in the fire insurance industry. In one of his forthright critical comments, Winter noted that in 1930 the fire insurers added a new rider to their basic policies. This additional feature, which later became known as Extended Coverage, provided protection against windstorm and a number of other common hazards. But having devised this needed and appealing product, the companies made little or no effort to exploit it. It was sold to some extent in the Middle West where tornadoes occur frequently, but otherwise the market was untapped.

Then in September, 1938, a hurricane devastated the northeastern section of the United States. When the wreckage was cleared away, it appeared that less than 10% of the losses had been covered by insurance. In other words, a coverage that had been on the market eight years had not been advertised and sold to the public. Again, in 1944, when another disastrous wind hit the Northeast, only 25% of the losses were covered. These were spectacular tests for the fire business. Winter thought it had been found wanting, and he said so.

There was not only a default in the obligation of the companies to furnish protection; there was another lesson apparent to those with vision. The old, established companies were leaving themselves wide open to competition from other types of insurers that were becoming more and more aggressive.

Winter was one of the practical visionaries who read this sign of the future accurately. He doggedly sought multiple line powers in order that his company, among others, would have a complete line of products to meet competition from other types of insurers that were going hammer and tongs after the mass market. He knew that the established companies would have to be able to offer, under one policy or a series of policies, protection against all the risks to which individuals and business enterprises were exposed. The success of the committee on which he served in achieving this goal came none too soon.

What amounted to a revolution shook the staid insurance business in the early 1950s. If the companies that were then put on the defensive had not been prepared to offer new and improved programs, the outcome would have been disastrous. As it was, because of their delayed start, they sustained severe inroads on their business and were forced into damaging practices to meet the competitive emergency.

And yet, this so-called revolution in insurance marketing that burst with full fury toward the end of Winter's active career had been perfectly apparent to him and other perceptive observers for years. They were not surprised when it came to a climax after World War II when a new market with unprecedented resources sprang up.

As early as the 1920s and the 1930s, organizations such as farm bureaus had set up insurance companies to provide inexpensive protection for their members. In the same era, one of the country's largest merchandising operations organized an insurer to sell policies through the mails, through booths in its stores and finally through employee-agents who worked exclusively for the company.

Using automobile insurance as a springboard, these companies were able from the start to sell below the costs of the traditional companies. The new operators carefully selected the customers to whom they sold automobile insurance. They centralized the handling of all the detail in connection with the insurance process: They prepared the policies, made out the bills and collected the premiums.

The innovators were successful from the start and gradually began to preempt the automobile market. By the time Tuttle and York took over the management of Atlantic at the end of 1952, the company and all others that operated along similar lines were threatened with the loss of additional business. The newcomers were not content with achieving a dominant place in automobile insurance sales. They began to apply their cost-cutting techniques to other personal business—such as homes and their contents. Finally, they began to invade the commercial market.

Alarmed at the prospect of losing more business in addition to

At Atlantic's Marine Library, students, historians, researchers and writers regularly consult the *Disaster Books*—the company's unique record of tragedies at sea on which part of this narrative is based.

automobile, the established insurers were shaken out of their complacency. Thanks to those who had fought long and hard for multiple line powers, these companies found that they had resources to combat the invaders. The first weapon they adopted was a new package of insurance called Homeowners. This included all the necessary personal coverage for different income groups.

The companies pushed the sale of this new product. Each sale meant that they had captured what amounted to an account. But some insurers went too far. In their zeal for volume, they not only granted overgenerous discounts but they were not too discriminating in their choice of customers. It was not too long before the effects were felt in heavy underwriting losses. At the same time, other lines of business, also subjected to rate cutting in the companies' quest for business, began to show losses.

This trend fed upon itself, and many companies began increasingly to depend on investments to salvage the losses they were sustaining in their fundamental business of insurance. This meant a completely unrestrained drive for premium volume to be placed in the investment market.

The trend was not easy to resist. But Tuttle and York, grounded in marine principles, made it clear that Atlantic was not going to abandon the philosophy under which the company had operated from its beginnings. They determined that underwriting was not to be sacrificed for volume.

In a particularly pertinent comment, York said: "We hope and expect to keep pace with changing trends in the industry and we are prepared to experiment where experimentation appears to serve the public and our policyholders. This shall include such subjects as new types of coverage, method of distribution, accounting and billing procedures, and so on, but shall not be limited to these.

"A willingness to change however does not encompass rate cutting. It is well to remember that the strategem of rate cutting per se has no place in the function of a constructive independent insurance underwriter. This is a device commonly resorted to by non-creative operators who have nothing of real value to add to the insurance standard."

York went on to point out that rate cutting more frequently than not weakens the position of the buyer's sole advocate in the insurance transaction—the independent agent or broker—a severe price for any buyer to pay.

He concluded by saying: "The Atlantic Companies need not and will not indulge in this practice. Where, in their independence of position they cannot improve upon something or some situation, they will sponsor and recommend the usual 'placement at market' and will seek the share thereof which their practiced integrity and industry have earned for them."

Tuttle has made some comments that complement York's. In a talk to Atlantic's officers and managers he analyzed the question of how large a company must be to hold its own and to progress in the modern market: "Large enough is of a sufficient size to compete successfully. But I like to think that our definition of 'large enough' goes a little further. I think we wish to be large enough to offer top quality insurance, to be able to pay our claims promptly and in full, and to be sold through quality sources. We wish to be large enough to pay quality people, those who are competent as insurance advisers, a proper compensation. We wish to attain a reasonable margin between what we take in and what we pay out."

These expressions of Tuttle and York were made in the early 1960s when the pell-mell race for premium volume by many companies continued unabated. It is interesting to compare their sentiments with those of the two earliest Atlantic presidents. Walter R. Jones, on being feted in 1853 for his accomplishments, set the company's goal as a "moderate favorable result hereafter." John D. Jones, on a similar occasion in 1892, when the trustees hailed him for reducing insurance to a science, told them that the company's prescription for success was hard work and incessant watchfulness.

Anyone interested in the continuity of Atlantic's operating principles must be impressed by the similarity of the views of its two most recent leaders to those of the first two.

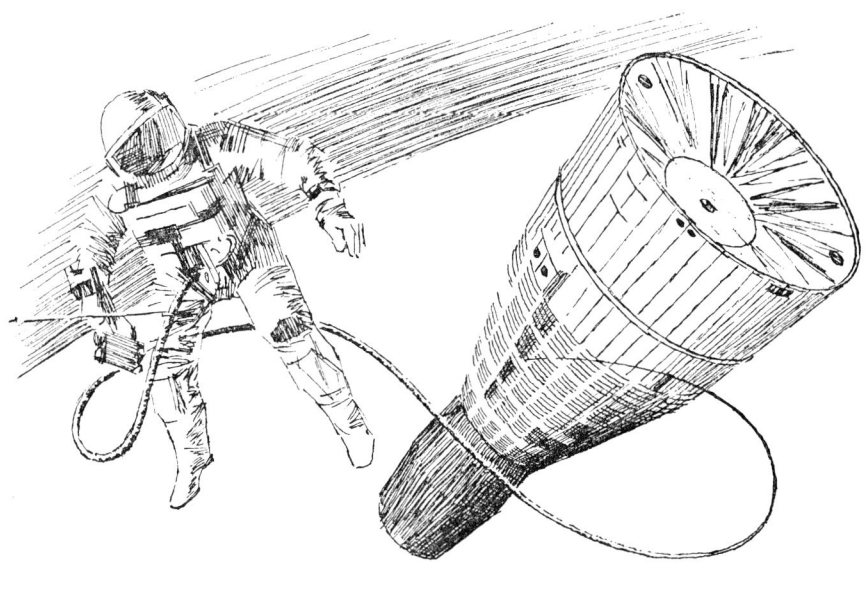

Times Change—Traditions Endure

Continuity in operating principles was not the only advantage Atlantic brought into a new and challenging period. Continuity in the character of its board of trustees was an equally important asset.

A third bulwark was the executive staff—both at New York headquarters and at the many other offices in the United States and in foreign countries. Over the years, as the insurance business became bigger and more complicated, Atlantic had decided that while administrative decisions were mainly reserved for the senior officers, their associates at many levels had to be entrusted with the shaping of operating policy and its execution. Management in depth was recognized as the key to continued progress as the insurance business moved out of the era when a company could bear the personal stamp of one or two individuals.

This precept was fortunately well established at Atlantic by the early 1950s when every aspect of social and commercial life had been transformed in less than a decade after the revolutionary arrival of the atomic age.

The country's population was rapidly heading toward 180 million—well above nine times the figure in 1842 when Atlantic was founded. High-speed expressways arrowed across the country. Suburbs sprang up in formerly inaccessible areas. Giant shopping centers followed. Television came into its own. Electronics and plastics became leading industries. Automation loomed large in plans for the future. Within a few years, satellites would be rocketed into orbit and the astronauts would follow in their wake.

The speed of the jet age was naturally reflected in the insurance business where competition, already severe, intensified at a bewildering pace. The merchandisers from other fields, who had formed insurers years before, now redoubled their efforts to preempt the mass market. The problem for traditional insurers was to adjust to the times or suffer steady attrition.

In adapting all phases of operation, Atlantic management had the continuing guidance and support of a board whose members were remarkably similar to their pioneer predecessors. Enterprise, financial acumen and willing participation in public affairs are characteristics that marked both the first trustees and the most recent. Among the first group were many whose venturesome spirit carried them from modest circumstances to leading roles in the mercantile, industrial and financial life of the country. This is no less true of their heirs at Atlantic's trustee table. Their affiliations in varied fields of business constitute a roster of quality organizations that have bolstered the American economy over a span of two centuries.

For example, Morris Nielsen, son of a Nebraska country doctor, started as a construction worker in 1924 in Chicago with The Babcock & Wilcox Company, one of the country's largest industrial firms. Under his direction, the company supplied thousands of boilers to the United States Navy and to merchant fleets in World War II. In 1954 he was elevated to vice-president, in 1957 he became the eighth president of the organization, and in 1965 he was elected chairman.

Active in harnessing atomic energy from the earliest days of nuclear development, Babcock & Wilcox designed, manufactured and installed the propulsion system of the Nuclear Ship *Savannah,* the world's first atomic merchant vessel.

A colleague of Mr. Nielsen on the board, J. Peter Grace, joined W. R. Grace & Co. after graduation from Yale University and within nine years became president of the company at the age of thirty-two. The investment community has witnessed the transformation of the company from a shipping line oriented toward Latin American trading and manufacturing into a major international chemical company with over 250 plants in 32 countries.

In directing these varied activities, which have more than quadrupled in scope in the past two decades, J. Peter Grace regularly visits dozens of countries in which his organization is active.

Born on a farm in North Carolina, Thomas A. Morgan worked during high school days as a carpenter, telephone lineman and powerplant helper before joining the United States Navy.

While serving as chief electrician on the U.S.S. *Delaware*, he met Elmer Sperry, an American inventor who had brought to the ship for testing purposes a new type of compass, revolutionary in concept because it was controlled by the earth's rotation instead of its magnetism. When the instrument proved defective in tests at sea, young Morgan took it apart, found the flaw and put the instrument into working condition.

After leaving the Navy he joined the Sperry firm as service engineer and became its chief executive, holding that post until his retirement in 1952. Under his direction, Sperry and its affiliates developed 140 new products, mainly in the fields of marine, aircraft and military equipment.

Railroad executive, college professor, Army engineer and shipping official are some of the roles John E. Slater has filled. He was with the Union Pacific Railroad and the New York, New Haven and Hartford Railroad Co. before he became professor of transportation at the University of Illinois.

From 1935 to 1956 he was executive vice-president and later president of American Export Lines, Inc. During the same period he organized and was the chief administrative officer of American Export Airlines, Inc. In World War II, as regional director for north and northwest Africa for the War Shipping Administration, he played a key role in supplying Allied war matériel in the Mediterranean combat area. For thirty-five years he was a partner of Coverdale & Colpitts, Consulting Engineers, New York, retiring in 1966 as senior partner.

The value to Atlantic of the scope and depth of these four trustees' experience is obvious. Even the challenges of the space age were hardly likely to daunt men whose careers have been spent with business enterprises that have endured and prospered through wars, depressions, recessions and the constantly shifting trends of the American economy. They absorbed the traditions of their firms, and Atlantic has been the beneficiary.

From its beginning, the company has profited by the counsel of trustees from the banking field. This has been especially true in recent years.

Since Atlantic's founding, The Bank of New York has been a neighbor on Wall Street. Appropriately, John C. Traphagen, retired chairman and president of the bank, has been a trustee of the insurer for thirty-six years.

Established 173 years ago by Alexander Hamilton, first Secretary of the Treasury, The Bank of New York opened its doors when New York's population was only 24,000. Thus, from the infancy of the United States, it has met the financial needs of New York and the nation.

An associate of Mr. Traphagen for many years and now executive vice-president and trustee of The Bank of New York, William R. Biggs, joined his former colleague on Atlantic's board in 1963.

His ability and reputation in financial circles are evidenced by some of the posts he has held: Investment adviser to the finance committee of the Ford Foundation, chairman of the executive committee and trustee of the Brookings Institution and a member of the board in a number of other corporations.

Another trustee, Benjamin Strong, is the descendant of a family with an unbroken record of participation in American financial affairs since the Revolution. Mr. Strong was chairman and president of

United States Trust Company of New York and is now a trustee of that firm. He represents the fifth generation of his family on Wall Street.

The first Benjamin Strong went to work there in 1783 at the age of thirteen. Five years later he became a clerk in the U. S. Treasury Department under Alexander Hamilton. Later he was named the second president of The Seamen's Bank for Savings.

The present Atlantic trustee began his business life as a trainee with National Bank of Commerce, and after executive experience with Bank of Manhattan he joined United States Trust in 1933. He became president in 1947.

When E. Roland Harriman was named an Atlantic trustee in 1954, the company inherited 136 years of banking and financial experience. Brown Brothers Harriman & Co., in which Mr. Harriman is a partner, was founded in 1818 and has been at the same site on Wall Street since 1833.

The son of E. H. Harriman, a name famous in railroading, E. Roland Harriman began his career with W. A. Harriman & Co. in New York and in 1927 formed the firm of Harriman Brothers & Co. with his brother Averell, who was governor of New York from 1954 to 1958 and who has long served the country in ambassadorial and other posts. The two Harriman firms were merged with Brown Brothers in 1931.

The Atlantic trustee is now also serving as chairman of Union Pacific Railroad.

The chief executive for many years of Atlantic's venerable neighbor, The Seamen's Bank for Savings, Clarence G. Michalis began his career as an engineer. He then became a public accountant and later went to Washington on a special assignment under Presidential appointment. He served in France during World War I.

During World War II he was head of American Relief for Holland, and in 1953 he was chairman of Holland Flood Relief, raising $1.5 million in less than three months. For these services he was decorated by the Dutch government. Mr. Michalis was a leading proponent of the formation of Atlantic's affiliate, Centennial, in 1942.

The positions held by Richard H. Mansfield in the banking and investment business have ranged from a clerkship to the presidency of Lazard Fund in New York.

He was in the securities department of the old Mechanics & Metals Bank for a short time before being made assistant manager of one of the branches. After the organization was merged into Chase National Bank, he managed one of the large offices until he was put in charge of the Rockefeller Center branch and elevated to vice-president.

The banking business of John D. Rockefeller, Jr., and his sons was handled under Mr. Mansfield's supervision, and the elder Rockefeller invited him to become senior financial adviser to the family. He also became vice-president of Rockefeller Center and executive vice-president and general manager of Rockefeller Brothers. After ten years in these posts he was named a general partner in Lazard Frères & Co., New York investment banking firm.

A great-grandson of J. P. Morgan, John P. Morgan 2nd is a vice-president of Morgan Guaranty Trust Company. His father, the late Junius S. Morgan, was an Atlantic trustee from 1947 to 1960.

Before entering business the present trustee was a lieutenant commander during World War II on antisubmarine vessels in both the Atlantic and Pacific theaters of war. He left active duty in 1946 and joined J. P. Morgan & Company. After the firm was merged in 1959 with Guaranty Trust, he was named vice-president in 1961.

The conservatism represented by banking has been joined with the innovation more suitable to other enterprises and with the wide knowledge of many aspects of business and public affairs brought to the trustee group by those long active in communications.

From the latter field came Marvin Pierce who, although holding an engineering degree from Massachusetts Institute of Technology, spent practically all of his working years in publishing. His first success in that field was with McCall Corp. He helped restore the organization to profitable operations after it had been in the red for eight years and remained thirty-six years, becoming president and chairman.

Later he was assistant to the publisher of *Time* magazine, then with Cowles Magazine & Broadcasting Co. as an adviser. He is now with International Executive Service Corps.

Alan H. Temple reversed the business pattern of Mr. Pierce. Mr. Temple was educated at Columbia University School of Journalism and was for a time an associate on the faculty. He joined the Theodore H. Price Publishing Co. in New York City as assistant editor of *Commerce & Finance* magazine, later advancing to managing editor and then to president.

His financial publishing background led him in 1931 into economic and public relations posts with First National City Bank, where he became executive vice-president and later vice-chairman. He continues as a member of the bank's trust board.

From the inception of the company, Atlantic trustees have not hesitated to relinquish their business interests when called upon for public service at many levels of government. A notable example in recent years is Raymond H. Fogler. He was an Atlantic trustee from 1943 to 1953 when he resigned to accept the office of Assistant Secretary of the Navy. On leaving Government service in 1957 he rejoined Atlantic's board.

Before he entered business, he was an instructor at Princeton and was a trustee of the University of Maine. He became president and a director of Montgomery Ward & Co., Inc., and for twelve years was president and general manager of W. T. Grant Company.

Another trustee who has distinguished himself in public service is Ellsworth Bunker. His first job was on the raw sugar docks in Yonkers, New York. He rose to the presidency of National Sugar Refining Company and later became chairman.

In 1951, Mr. Bunker terminated his business career by accepting an appointment as United States Ambassador to Argentina, where he served one year. He was then named Ambassador to Italy.

In 1954, he became president of the American Red Cross and directed the relief and rehabilitation operations during the flood disasters in California and New England.

In 1956, President Eisenhower appointed Mr. Bunker Ambassador to India, and he was given a leave of absence from Atlantic's board for more than four years. At the time, he was also a United States Delegate to the Eleventh General Assembly of the United Nations.

While he was Ambassador to India, he temporarily held the same rank in Nepal. In 1962 he acted as mediator on behalf of the United Nations in the dispute between Indonesia and the Netherlands over West New Guinea. The following year he negotiated a disengagement agreement in Yemen between Saudi Arabia and the United Arab Republic. Later he became Ambassador to the Organization of American States and now holds the distinguished position of Ambassador at Large.

Most trustees "take a seat" on Atlantic's board, but when he became a member in 1929, John B. Clark upset that practice. Only thirty years old at the time, he was somewhat diffident in the company of his veteran colleagues. He selected a chair a little apart from the distinguished group, but, unfortunately, his choice was one of Atlantic's famed horsehair antiques, which promptly splintered and deposited him on the board-room floor. This disconcerting introduction might have been dismaying but not to a young man who had been a pilot in the Army Air Force in France and whose motto from the beginning of his career was "getting up above the crowd."

Mr. Clark had a brief career in banking before joining the Clark Thread Co., founded in 1812. Clark thread is not only a byword in business annals, but the name is familiar to every woman who has ever plied a needle. In the company's early days, the supply of flax from Europe was cut off because of the Napoleonic Wars. With the textile industry threatened, the Clark family devised a method of substituting cotton for flax and a thriving new industry was born.

John B. Clark was for many years president of the company and later of its successor, Coats & Clark, Inc., of which he now is honorary chairman. For thirty-eight years he has contributed with distinction to Atlantic management.

George M. Schurman, descendant of a family that came to America from the Netherlands in the 1640s, became active in the manufacture of textile bags after military service in World War I. He started with Riegel Sack Co. and later joined National Bag Corp., of which he became the principal owner. During World War II, Mr. Schurman was on a number of industry advisory committees of the War Production Board and the Office of Price Administration in Washington.

Among the trustees representing one of the fastest-growing modern industries is Robert B. Semple.

After eleven years in various research, development and sales assignments with Monsanto Chemical Company, he became director of the firm's general development department in 1944. In 1949 he joined the Wyandotte Chemicals Corporation as president.

William B. Rand was with Air Reduction Sales Co. before service in World War II as a lieutenant colonel.

He then joined United States Lines Company as assistant to the general manager of the operating department. He was elected executive vice-president in 1960 and president in 1961. In the same year he took his place on Atlantic's board.

As president of The Mutual Life Insurance Company of New York, Roger Hull brought to Atlantic's councils in 1963 valuable knowledge from an allied field of business.

Mr. Hull's entire career has been with Mutual of New York. Beginning in 1928 as an agent in Meridian, Mississippi, he progressed to vice-president and manager of agencies in 1941, to executive vice-president and trustee in 1950 and to president in 1959.

From an organization steeped in the lore of American business, J. Wilson Newman, chairman of Dun & Bradstreet, Inc., came to Atlantic's board in 1960.

He began his career with R. G. Dun & Co. in 1931 shortly before its merger with the Bradstreet Co. He was made a vice-president in 1946, president in 1952, and in 1960, chairman and chief executive of the firm which is paramount in evaluating and rating organizations in every commercial field.

Appropriately, the newest addition to Atlantic's board represents one of the most modern and fastest growing of American business activities—the airlines. Marion Sadler, who became a trustee in 1966, was a teacher before joining American Airlines in 1941.

He held responsible posts in key cities and at New York headquarters before becoming director of passenger sales in 1955. He moved up to vice-president in charge of customer service in 1957, to vice-president and general manager in 1959 and to president in 1964.

The top officials of Atlantic are, of course, also on the board. Two executives, hitherto unmentioned in this narrative, have served many years with distinction both as company officers and as trustees: Dale E. Taylor and Herriot Small.

Mr. Taylor, who will complete his third decade with Atlantic in 1967, became an assistant secretary in 1947 and in 1951 was transferred to the Midwest division as assistant general manager. Four years later he returned to the home office as vice-president in charge of ocean marine operations, and in 1959 he was elevated to executive vice-president.

He has represented the company in numerous marine organizations. His industry posts include: Manager of American Hull Insurance Syndicate; chairman of Cargo Reinsurance Association; governor of Foreign Credit Insurance Association; president of Yacht Safety Bureau and second vice-president of American Institute of Marine Underwriters.

Herriot Small was with Balfour, Guthrie & Co., Ltd. from 1917 to 1945. His father was a founder of the marine department of that company.

Mr. Small joined Atlantic in 1946 in the San Francisco office. He succeeded Miles F. York as vice-president and general manager of the Pacific division in 1951 when Mr. York moved to the home office to become executive vice-president.

Mr. Small was long prominent in marine circles on the Pacific Coast. He was president of the Board of Marine Underwriters from 1944 to 1946, president of Association of Marine Underwriters of San Francisco, and chairman of the Pacific Advisory Committee of the American Cargo War Risk Reinsurance Exchange.

He retired at the end of 1963 but remains on the board.

The combination of careers in widely disparate fields—as exemplified in the foregoing review of board members—brought to bear on

Atlantic's problems the broadest variety of insights at a time when they were most urgently needed. Every business represented by the trustees from other fields was affected by the transformation in the American economy—before the insurance industry felt the impact of change.

As the leaders of their own organizations, Atlantic trustees had long experience in adapting their enterprises to modern demands. Their counsel therefore provided a cushion of confidence to Atlantic management and was a primary factor in the company's orderly approach to the task of coping with a new insurance era.

This approach was not based on hasty adoption of random changes but on gradual acceleration of established methods to achieve continued growth. These methods included upgrading of the staff and addition of men with management potential; closer relations with the independent sales force through formal conferences and regular interchange of views; innovation in products by development of new coverages and adaptation of time-tested policies to modern needs; aggressive advertising to supplement intensified marketing programs and effective communications with all who had a stake in the company's success.

In the early 1950s some insurers were tempted to seek short cuts in their efforts to keep abreast of competition. Some thought that the immediate transfer of all procedures to computers and other electronic devices was the basic answer to new problems. While it was one of the first companies to adopt modern data processing, Atlantic concluded that no mechanical procedures could be any more effective than the manpower behind them. The fundamental need then was not new machines, methods and procedures—vital as these were—but additional men with varied talents who could be grounded in Atlantic precepts, technically trained, given experience at the company's numerous branches and thus developed into the flexible type of managers indispensable to company growth.

Atlantic went after this objective by setting up an administrative training program. Each year the company recruits college graduates and other men with business experience. Their average age in recent years has been twenty-seven. The class is also open to present staff members.

The recruits spend mornings at the College of Insurance of the Insurance Society of New York. In the afternoon, they attend company classes. This division of studies gives the men a grasp of the principles of all phases of the business and an understanding of Atlantic's specific application of these fundamentals.

Toward the end of training, the men are asked to express a preference for the activity that they think will bring out the best of their capabilities. While a trainee may not be able to answer this question, he is at least encouraged to think hard about it. This procedure highlights the change in company philosophy since the days when young men like Winter were told to follow orders and leave all the thinking to those in top management.

After training, the men are relocated around the country and are on their way to realizing the many opportunities in field work, underwriting, claims, electronics, branch management and other specialties.

Aware that development of internal manpower was only one necessary phase of preparation for growth, Atlantic management began cooperative planning with independent producers as another major activity. The company recognized that its salesmen, who set the insurance process in motion by producing premiums from quality business, must share management's confidence from the inception of all important projects.

Atlantic formalized this conviction in 1959 when it departed from the traditional trial-and-error method of introducing new products. The company concluded that with competition mounting it was unrealistic to make home-office decisions on what coverages would sell and then expect its agents to market them.

Accordingly, as a first step, a questionnaire on commercial property protection was sent to 600 selected producers, soliciting their help in creating a new product. Largely on the basis of the answers, the Retailers Safeguard policy was designed and introduced in several states. Producers' ideas helped to make this package of protection an immediate success.

The practical results of this experiment encouraged the company to arrange a series of informal seminars with producers. These gatherings were not merely a vehicle to convey company ideas; Atlantic's independent representatives were given full opportunity to express their opinions. Topics for the sessions were left to the discretion of agents. However, a unifying theme was adopted: "What should we—company and agents—be doing to meet today's intense competition?"

Many important decisions were based on the findings, and in 1961 Atlantic decided to expand the program. The ideal agency-company council would be one in which all the company's agents could confer with executives and consider common problems. Since this was obviously impractical, Atlantic adopted the best possible alternative. This was the establishment of a National Council of producers and three regional units. Each year there are meetings of the Pacific, Midwest and Eastern councils, followed by sessions of the national group. This arrangement assures full consideration of the specialized problems agents encounter in different geographic areas.

Care was taken to have representatives from both large and small agencies, for the questions they must solve differ in degree. To obtain the necessary variety of views, Atlantic chose professional producers from big cities, small towns and suburban areas. This planning of the make-up of the discussion groups insured the broadest cross section of agency opinion in all markets, which is the most valuable feature of the councils.

Atlantic attaches such importance to the program that the National Council has been asked to regard itself as a committee of the board of trustees.

Since its agents serve on a rotating basis on the councils, Atlantic is fast building a backlog of fully informed producers who, through consultation with management on every phase of operations, are aided in delivering the professional service the company advocates. In turn, Atlantic is kept in close touch with the market by those who know it best and is able to stay on top of rapidly changing developments.

Atlantic's rapport and cooperation with its agents is all the more remarkable when it is recalled that during its first ninety years the company wrote only ocean marine business that came almost entirely from specialized producers on the eastern seaboard—mainly in New York, Philadelphia and Boston. The company's competitors had a long lead in other classes of insurance and in building agency representation countrywide.

However, from its inception, Atlantic was a "middleman's" company. In 1845, two of its employees founded Johnson & Higgins—the country's oldest insurance brokerage firm. Thus, although Atlantic was late in joining the expansion of the independent production system, when it did so, it was with full understanding of and dedication to the principles involved. The vital role of the agents' councils in the company's current operation is sufficient testimony.

Upgrading of its internal manpower and continuing consultation with its independent sales organization were the two basic steps Atlantic took to gear itself for modern marketing demands. These came with bewildering rapidity, posing challenges that underwriters had never before been called upon to face. Not only were new products needed but traditional coverages had to be made more flexible to meet unique demands.

In the mid-1950's insurers were asked to provide protection for large nuclear installations and the enormous liability inherent in atomic activities. Never in history had risks with greater loss potential been presented. Insurers accepted their obligation by combining their resources and talents and writing this business under pooling arrangements in which Atlantic participates. This business originates with agents and brokers and flows to the pools through the usual production channels—an outstanding example of the independent system's primacy in supplying the most vital coverage needs of the country.

A great deal of the expansion in Atlantic protection has been accomplished by adaptation of some of the company's oldest coverages. Transportation policies, for example, were the basic product Atlantic offered when it began operations, but the underwriters of 1842 could not possibly have imagined the scope this business would achieve. One of Atlantic's largest risks in recent times has been the Army and Air Force Exchange Service, more commonly known as the PX system. Every item the system buys, ships and sells overseas is insured by Atlantic against the risks of transportation in all types of conveyances from the moment of leaving the manufacturer's plant until delivery for distribution to military men and their families.

PX transmission lines stretch to Vietnam, from Texas to Turkey, from Kansas to Korea, from Oklahoma to Okinawa, and to the offshore bases that guard approaches to East Coast ports of the United States.

WALTER R. JONES
1842-1855

JOHN D. JONES
1855-1895

WILLIAM H. H. MOORE
1895-1897

ANTON A. RAVEN
1897-1915

CORNELIUS ELDERT
1915-1930

WALTER W. PARSONS
1930-1934

WILLIAM D. WINTER
1934-1946

J. ARTHUR BOGARDUS
1946-1951

FRANKLIN B. TUTTLE
1951-1953

MILES F. YORK
1953-1966

DAVID A. FLOREEN
1966-

For 125 years, eleven men have served as president of Atlantic Mutual.

Goods that are sped with Atlantic protection help to meet basic needs and to provide some of the comforts of home to those in the services of their country as far away as 10,000 miles.

Atlantic's continuing role as a transportation insurer was even more dramatically illustrated in one of the greatest air disasters in history.

Late in 1960, two giant airliners—a TWA Super Constellation and a United Air Lines DC-8—were approaching their New York destinations. The TWA plane, out of Dayton, Ohio, was bound for La Guardia Airport; the United flight from Chicago was headed for International, now Kennedy, Airport.

Within minutes of their scheduled landings, the planes collided near Miller Army Air Field on Staten Island. The Constellation fell to the field, but the DC-8 wobbled over the water to Brooklyn and crashed in a busy neighborhood. All 128 occupants of both planes and six persons on the ground in Brooklyn were killed. Atlantic was an insurer of cargo on the DC-8. This included mink pelts. Strewn about the wreckage, they added a pathetic note of finery to the shabby street where the DC-8 crashed.

Atlantic's involvement in this grim episode was in a sense inevitable. The company had foreseen and had studied the rapid growth of cargo transportation by air. Beginning in 1952, air freight had increased more than 200% by the early 1960s. As a pioneer protector of cargo, Atlantic was in the forefront of underwriters ready to assume air risks.

The United States in the jet age is only 5½ hours wide and 2½ hours deep. The entire country is a suburban-like market. The rest of the world is right next door—24 hours away at most. Inevitably, there has been a boom in cargo transportation by air, and Atlantic has kept pace. Thus, somewhat ironically, many of the world's newest businesses depend on one of the world's oldest—marine insurance—to safeguard their shipments under the most ancient of all contracts, the Open Cargo policy.

To some, the centuries-old marine policy may seem to be notable only for its romantic wording:

"Touching the adventures and perils which we, the said underwriters are contented to bear and take upon us, they are of the seas, men-of-war, fire, lightning, earthquake, enemies, pirates, rovers, assailing thieves, jettisons, letters of mart and counter-mart, surprisals, takings at sea, arrest, restraints and detainments of all kings, princes, and peoples of what nation, condition or quality soever, barratry of the master and mariners, and of all other like perils, losses and misfortunes that have or shall come to the hurt, detriment, or damage of the said vessel or any part thereof."

But this language, still appearing in today's marine covers, is more than merely picturesque. It reveals that marine underwriters had a package policy hundreds of years before the so-called modern forms were on the market.

In recent years Atlantic, of course, developed many packaged plans, which furnish all the essential property and liability coverages. These include Homeowners; the Safeguard Program for various types of business; comprehensive policies for manufacturers and industrial interests and packages for apartments, office buildings and other risks. But Atlantic's eminence in the package field was not solely a modern development; it had its roots in the last century when the company first supplied protection on the all-risk marine basis. The application of marine precepts to other lines was a logical step. After all, Winter had based his long fight for multiple line underwriting on the extension of marine procedures, and there should be little cause for wonder that the company was in the forefront of insurers offering the "latter-day" packages.

While it is dedicated to innovation, Atlantic believes that the chief merits of its newest products lie in the oldest of insurance values, which is built into them: The marine philosophy. Simply stated, this means that the insured must be served first; that he must be provided with protection that is as complete as possible, that he must have the services of a professional agent or broker and that claims must be paid promptly and ungrudgingly.

The competitive struggle of the past fifteen years was and is largely a contest for public favor between independent agents who represent Atlantic in addition to similar companies, and other producers who sell exclusively for a single organization. In recent years, therefore, traditional insurers in their advertising have emphasized the superior services of their independent representatives.

This was not a new concept to Atlantic, which had long publicly promoted the performance of its producers. Shortly after the exclusive-agent companies began to step up their activities in the 1930s, the company mounted an advertising counterattack with the independent agent as the spearhead. The company chose newspapers as the best advertising battleground from the agents' standpoint.

From the start of this program in 1936, Atlantic deemphasized its own name, stressing the performance and the value of the independent middleman.

Believing that its advertising would be fully effective only if potential clients were aided in comprehending the fundamental facts about the products it offers, Atlantic later sponsored an informative series on what buyers should know.

Since a vital part of any salesman's service is the company that stands behind the product he offers, Atlantic has emphasized this point through the years while continuing to feature its producers. Through a cooperative newspaper advertising campaign initiated in the early 1960s, the company brought this message to prospective buyers: Men of Judgment Buy Atlantic Insurance; Men of Integrity Sell It. In 1964 alone, this effective statement was used in 120 newspapers with a combined readership of more than 70 million.

Finally, to underscore the philosophy of operation that management has insisted on preserving, Atlantic in 1965 and 1966 rounded out its advertising by a campaign based on famous episodes from the company's history. These advertisements demonstrated how Atlantic has maintained its marine traditions and how it has applied them to the modern insurance market. The dramatic colored illustrations in this narrative were adapted from this advertising program.

The New York Times gave unusual prominence to this campaign in a feature story that included these comments:

"Depicting disaster at sea is not the usual tack taken by marine insurance companies in their advertising and promotion approach. As a rule, they feature sunny, placid seascapes where a hard wind rarely blows.

"But Atlantic has decided to call a storm a storm and a disaster a disaster."

The *Times* writer was perceptive. The very title of this 125-year character sketch of the company—*Gray Days and Gold*—is prime evidence of management's insistence on presenting a realistic picture of its affairs.

This insistence has been carried over into the company's overall information program. This is not a noisy, overblown activity in which success is judged by the volume of bulletins and news releases put into circulation. Management rather regards communications as the transfer of understanding from one mind to another. One method used to achieve this aim was a questionnaire directed to 546 participants in Atlantic education programs, asking them what they wished to know. The questions most frequently asked were: "What Are We Doing?"—"Where Are We Going?"—"What Goes On?"

Forthright answers were given by top officials of the company in a series of meetings with employees.

Atlantic follows the same candid communications course in its reports to policyholders and in the systematic provision of news of its affairs to the insurance and financial communities.

The company's continuing information program is primarily carried out in the aptly named monthly publication, the *Atlantic Log*. The *Log* reports on current problems and explains plans to meet them. It links the organization in human interest terms by recording employee activities, promotions and achievements.

Employees are given a sense of belonging, not by paternalistic messages from management, but by presentation of pertinent facts. For example, shortly after annual results are available each year, the *Log* carries a detailed account of how the company has fared. Interim results are published on the same basis so that the staff has a continuing grasp of how their company is progressing.

Feature stories in the *Log* describe the inner workings of each main department and even of specific jobs, such as the underwriter, special agent, adjuster, branch manager and others. There is no longer any mystery about any Atlantic activity.

Challenge and Opportunity

The wisdom of the course taken by successive waves of management in the distant past can be assessed because the passing years clearly reveal the long-term consequences. Not so easily measured are the results of the decisions made by management in dealing with current conditions.

And yet, the effect of the most recent Atlantic administration approach in coping with a transformed business can be gauged from the end of 1953 to the end of 1965—a rather respectable period for comparative purposes.

The record reveals the results of the orderly program of augmenting and upgrading the staff; of a closer alliance with independent producers; of the development of new products and adaptations of the old; of aggressive advertising and finally of forthright communications that keep all parties to the enterprise fully informed at all times.

Operating under these guidelines, Atlantic employees at every level and the company's producers brought the organization to new heights. This is succinctly illustrated by a comparison of significant figures for the period in question:

(Figures in thousands)

	Assets	Surplus	Net Premiums Written
1953	$ 59,767	$18,612	$25,862
1965	$155,604	$42,697	$70,681

Even this encouraging pattern does not tell the entire story. The company's competitors have also shown rapid growth in the years in question. However, a great many of them have resorted to large-scale public financing. Atlantic's development has all been financed from within.

While the country's gross national product at the end of 1965 had increased approximately 85% over the figure for 1953, Atlantic's gross premium volume had risen 153%. Growth in terms of size, however, is but one barometer and not the most important consideration in Atlantic's estimation, although it regards the steady addition of quality business as imperative. A more meaningful measure of company achievement in the years of upheaval in the industry was the attainment of an underwriting profit in all but three years from 1953 to 1965.

This was no mean feat in an era when both internal and external factors made profits elusive. Rate cutting not only persisted in practically all lines but indiscriminately broadened coverage was granted at the increasingly inadequate prices. Added to this self-inflicted burden on the insurance business was an inflationary trend that further aggravated the disproportion between the premiums companies took in and the claims they paid out.

Furthermore, there was another factor with which even the most intelligent insurance management was in no position to cope: Nature. From the early 1950s insurers were plagued by hurricanes. Three of these feminine furies—Carol, Edna and Hazel—devastated the eastern seaboard in 1954 and brought Atlantic losses of $3.5 million. In the next year, Diane swept through Pennsylvania, New Jersey, New York and New England with devastating floods in her wake. In 1956 Atlantic had a variety of substantial losses: The sinking of the *Andrea Doria,* the collision of two airliners over the Grand Canyon, forest fires on the Pacific Coast and the Luckenbach pier conflagration in Brooklyn, New York.

In 1957, Hurricane Audrey took over where her predecessors had left off, causing widespread damage in Louisiana and Texas. Donna played the leading destructive role in 1960 in the Caribbean and the eastern United States, and in 1961 Carla repeated Audrey's pattern.

But all of these cataclysms were but pale forerunners of Betsy, hitherto mentioned as the cause of the greatest loss in insurance history. Atlantic's share of the havoc she caused in 1965 was about $2 million.

Atlantic does not deplore its financial outlays in sharing the cost of tragedies. The management rather lays stress on the part it was privileged to play as a private insurer in alleviating the distress of hundreds of thousands of those stricken and in restoring the economic prosperity of the areas involved. Atlantic believes that the essential value of its products is best demonstrated by the benefits distributed to those who have sought the company's protection.

While coping with the persistent competitive problems of the years between 1953 and 1966 and with the menacing situation posed by mounting losses in virtually all classes of business, management proceeded with another primary responsibility: Planning and gearing its operations for the future.

A move basic to expansion was made in 1956 when Atlantic sold to Metropolitan Life Insurance Co. the property at Wall and William streets where its first home office had been located and where it continued to do business. The stately old Building of the Ships and the adjacent United States Trust Co. structure were razed in preparation for the erection of today's twenty-seven-story Atlantic Building. While dismantling and construction were proceeding, the company made its headquarters in the John Wanamaker Building where, forty-four years before, David Sarnoff in his telegrapher's cubicle on the roof had received and relayed messages on the sinking of the *Titanic*.

In the fall of 1959, the staff came home to the new headquarters. A time capsule had been set in the eleventh floor of the building by Tuttle and York. This contained the predictions of insurance editors concerning the state of the business a century hence, copies of the leading New York City newspapers, issues of the *Atlantic Log,* and memorabilia of the year 1959.

As the company entered another decade and completed its first full year in 1960 in the modern structure at the legendary location, it was fitting that assets crossed the $100 million mark for the first time and reached $102,755,000.

Meanwhile, additions were steadily being made to the countrywide network of offices in order to bring to the company's producers and policyholders its complete services in strategic market locations. By the end of the period covered in this narrative, Atlantic had four divisional offices and thirty-one branches and was doing business from one end of the country to the other, including Alaska and Hawaii.

Since increased premium volume from abroad is a primary factor in the company's projections for sound growth, expansion was not limited to the United States. In keeping with the growing importance of international operations, Atlantic augmented its foreign activities by acquiring three insurance companies: The Sea of Holland, Fire Insurance Company of Canada and Unión de Seguros S.A. of Mexico. The company also has an important agency in London and through reinsurance treaties participates in worldwide markets.

In 1962 Atlantic marked its 120th anniversary. Although this occurred during what might fairly be described as the most turbulent period in insurance history, the company had a net operating gain of $3,174,000 for the year—the largest the organization ever achieved. Total premiums had increased much faster proportionately than had the agency plant, and the volume of business written per employee was twice that of a decade ago—a direct reflection of the value of Atlantic's strategy in concentrating on manpower improvement, training programs and closer relations with the sales force.

However, as if in confirmation of the adage that history repeats itself, the year was followed by one of substantial losses, just as the year 1853, when Walter Restored Jones was feted for his successful conduct of the company, was succeeded by the disasters of 1854 and the low point in Atlantic's history.

The results of 1963 marked the beginning of a particularly adverse loss cycle for the entire business. In the next two years, practically every insurer suffered steady attrition from the underpriced homeowners and automobile classes, which constitute a large share of premium writings. This relentless drain made 1964 the worst year for property-liability underwriters since World War I—a dubious distinction soon preempted by 1965, which was marked by an unusual number of catastrophes, culminating in Betsy. Particularly significant to Atlantic were the severe marine losses sustained by the industry in both years.

As had happened so often in the past, a change in Atlantic's administration coincided with a critical period in the business. In late 1966, Tuttle retired as chairman and chief executive officer after thirty-five years of distinguished service. York succeeded him in the top posts, and David A. Floreen, who had been brought to New York headquarters two years before in preparation for these management maneuvers, was named the eleventh president of the company.

Tuttle had joined Atlantic in the depths of the depression and at a time when the company's growth had been stymied since the turn of the century. Yet, in his three-and-a-half decades at Wall and William streets, he saw the premium volume expand by almost twenty-three times the $3.1 million figure that was written when Winter and Bogardus engaged him to make the company a factor in the inland marine business.

He not only fulfilled this assignment but soon moved into administrative duties, leading to the presidency from 1951 to 1953 and to the chairmanship from the latter year until his retirement. He was an officer for thirty-one of his almost thirty-five years of service and a trustee for twenty years. York has characterized Tuttle as the architect of Atlantic's expansion beyond the marine field into the inland marine, fire and casualty business.

Tuttle also filled a traditional role of Atlantic executives by serving as president of Life Saving Benevolent Association. He was for years a director of the Insurance Society of New York, holding various offices, and was the first to fill the newly created post of chairman of its board.

York had been with Atlantic twenty-two years—thirteen as president—when he became chairman. His role as leader of the company's expansion in the past decade had been foreshadowed by his success in his early days with Atlantic in organizing Pacific Coast operations.

York's expansionist outlook and his energy were demonstrated by the number of industry posts he held while discharging his primary duties as Atlantic's president. He has been president and a director of American Institute of Marine Underwriters and of Association of Marine Underwriters of the United States, as well as manager and vice-chairman of American Hull Insurance Syndicate and a director and vice-president of United States Salvage Association. He is a manager of the American Bureau of Shipping and is on its standing and finance committees. York was also the ninth of ten Atlantic presidents to head the Board of Underwriters of New York, a marine organization founded in 1820.

Tuttle and York had many complementary qualities—as did Bogardus and Winter. In the latter's phrase, they too were "alike enough and yet different enough." In some respects they were exactly alike, notably in their concept of management as a function that had to be increasingly shared. In their view, the ideal administrator was distinguished by his willingness and skill in delegating responsibility and authority.

This concord between the two top officials led to their selection and recommendation of Floreen, who had demonstrated these qualities, for the presidency. A native of Chicago, he began his career there in 1934 with the Automobile Insurance Company of Hartford. He was later marine manager at Detroit for Home of New York before joining Atlantic in 1946.

For almost fifteen years he was in charge of operations in Texas and the Southwest. As branch manager at Houston, he supervised a territory of more than 476,000 square miles. His delegation of managerial responsibility to six key men was a primary factor in the success of operations in the Southwest during his tenure.

His performance there led to Floreen's appointment in 1960 as president of the affiliated Unión de Seguros S.A., one of the oldest insurers in Mexico. Outstanding results recorded by the company provided further evidence of leadership—on a much broader scale—and brought Floreen to the home office late in 1964 as assistant to York. He was named senior executive vice-president early in 1965.

Rounding out the top administrative staff were Maurice D. Stack, who was named chairman of the finance committee and chief financial officer, and Harold A. Eckmann, who became senior executive vice-president and a trustee.

Mr. Stack began his career in 1946 in the investment department of the Carnegie Corporation of New York. In 1948 he joined Teachers Insurance & Annuity Association, an organization founded by Carnegie Corporation. From 1949 to 1954 he was with First National Bank of New York.

He came to Atlantic in 1954 as financial secretary and was elected financial vice-president in 1957 and a trustee in 1961. He is treasurer and a member of the board of managers of Life Saving Benevolent Association and a trustee of Union Square Savings Bank.

Mr. Eckmann's insurance experience before he joined Atlantic in 1949 included service with the well-known brokerage firm of Johnson & Higgins.

He successfully conducted Atlantic's branch at Charlotte, North Carolina, from 1957 to 1960, when he was recalled to the home office. In 1962 he was named a vice-president and was given responsibility for the New York metropolitan division.

Smooth transition and continuity, rather than abrupt change, thus marked the accession of the new administration at the end of 1966. As chairman, York had behind him the eventful years in the presidency during which he promoted Atlantic's greatest growth. Floreen not only had varied experience in many phases of the business but had also been president of a company and had been at headquarters for intensive grooming in the two preceding years.

Under the leadership of these two men, Atlantic moved toward the years ahead. They assumed new roles when the entire business was enduring a severe trial, and they had no illusions about the difficulty of meeting unending problems.

However, they had no intention of allowing adverse circumstances to cloud their projections for the future. This was illustrated when York answered the staff's question of "Where Are We Going?" by citing the consistent yearly growth rate of 10% and indicating his confidence that this would continue.

His optimism is well grounded. The record of the company's first century and a quarter is overwhelmingly an encouraging one, however harsh may have been some of its experiences in adverse years and however uncertain the future has always been at any juncture.

Accomplishments thus far, then, may justifiably be regarded as harbingers of what is to come, as Atlantic continues to innovate and to seek improvement. The company's management in the past—in good times and bad—has always been marked by courage. And the courageous company, like the courageous individual, is not dismayed by the threat of uncertainties ahead but recognizes and welcomes them as greater opportunities cloaked in the guise of challenge.

Reference Sources

The Enterprising Americans—John Chamberlain
Harper & Row 1961

When the Guns Roared—Philip Van Doren Stern
Doubleday & Co. 1965

Sarnoff—Eugene Lyons
Harper & Row 1965

The Rise of New York Port—Robert G. Albion
Charles Scribner's Sons 1939

Valentine's *Manual of Old New York, 1919*

Atlantic Log—Official employee
   publication of Atlantic Mutual Insurance Company

The Hartford of Hartford—Hawthorne Daniel
Random House 1960

Biography of a Business—Marquis James
Bobbs-Merrill 1942
(History of Insurance Company of North America)

Ninety Years of Marine Insurance
Atlantic Mutual Insurance Company 1932

Many Men—One Purpose
Atlantic Mutual Insurance Company 1947

Marine Insurance—William D. Winter
McGraw-Hill Book Co., revised edition, 1952

Disaster Books—Official records of tragedies at sea
   maintained by Atlantic Mutual Insurance Company